The Wounded Healer

A Guide to Revealing the Purpose for the Pain

HEATHER BARFIELD

Paperback ISBN: 978-1-970079-84-5
eBook ISBN: 978-1-63616-098-6

Published By Opportune Independent Publishing Company

Edited by Speak Write Play, LLC

Printed in the United States of America
For permission requests, email the publisher with the subject line as "Attention: Permissions Coordinator" to the email address below:

info@opportunepublishing.com
www. opportunepublishing.com

Dedication

This book is dedicated to all wounded healers everywhere. No one knows the cost of the anointing of God on your life. Stand strong and continue to allow the Lord to use you for His glory and purpose.

Contents

Foreword   9

Acknowledgments   13

Introduction   15

Chapter 1: Surrender   19

Chapter 2: Pray About Everything   25

Chapter 3: God's Pruning   33

Chapter 4: Bearing Fruit   41

Chapter 5: The Purposes of God   47

Chapter 6: Walk in Faith   51

Chapter 7: It's Not About You   63

Chapter 8: Peace in the Storm   71

Chapter 9: A New Season   77

Chapter 10: God Heals the Brokenhearted   83

Chapter 11: The Power of Forgiveness   101

Chapter 12: The Wounded Healer   107

Closing Thoughts   119

About the Author   121

Foreword

In 2016, I was asked to host an event and perform a spoken word poem at my church. After my performance, an energetic and spunky woman came to the pew I was sitting in to talk to me, and I recognized her as Pastor Heather Barfield. She was a familiar face, which I'd seen active in the community and as a guest speaker at many events and services but never had the pleasure of formally meeting. She skipped the formality and sometimes awkwardness of first meetings and connected with me as if we had known each other for years, speaking candidly about her independent ministry, Daughters of Destiny. She had gotten the bright idea not only to invite me to the annual conference taking place the next month but to ask me to host it. I had experienced hosting events as a locally known poet, MC, and guest speaker, but it still felt like a tall order. Nevertheless, I said "yes" to the offer and looked forward to attending.

I expected the Daughter of Destiny Conference to be a run-of-the-mill, "church outside of church" event—a packed lineup of female guest speakers preaching for an hour or more about women's empowerment, self-love, and living your best life (with God, of course). However, the more I listened on, it felt less like a conference and more like a safe space for women who had been through trials and tribulations to bare themselves and boldly share their experiences. Some of their lives had come full circle while others were still in transition, but their guards were down, and they were ministering from a place of vulnerability, something I wasn't used to seeing. After that first conference, it was a no-brainer for me to stay connected with Pastor Barfield and Daughters of Destiny; every conference thereafter upheld the spirit of transparency, and the essence of her life's work and character permeated through her ministry.

That very essence of transparency flows throughout *The Wounded Healer.* As an established author, Pastor Barfield reaches deep beyond devotion and the formalities of ministry to the most familiar place she knows—her own life. She walks us through many of her most pivotal moments, tracing every decision back to the intentional prayers she prayed to God for clarity and direction. She confirms God's steering over decisions that led to the most difficult seasons of her life and ponders the questions we all may ask when facing hardship: God, how could you lead me here? Is this really of your doing? I empathize with how relatable these questions are, especially for young women like myself, charting out the course of our lives and reeling from the consequences of decisions made in counsel with God. It's extremely hard to fathom that saying "yes" to His plan for our lives and trusting Him every step of the way sometimes yields unfavorable results, but staying the course produces endurance and purpose.

As a millennial, many of the sentiments expressed in this book have mirrored my own feelings, and I implore readers, especially young women, to draw connections to their own lives and be reminded that God uses our experiences to qualify us for our purpose. If we fully trust Him, He will take us through, but in the process, He builds us up to be unstoppable forces with compassion and wisdom. In 2016, I met the finished product of God's refinement in Pastor Barfield and the Daughters of Destiny Ministry that has transformed the lives of many. *The Wounded Healer* is her origin story—the qualifier for a life of purpose. Be encouraged.

—Latoya Barfield

Acknowledgments

I want to give thanks and acknowledgment to:

My sons, Justin and Nilee, for their consistent mercy, kindness, and love toward their parents and for their graceful entrance into manhood as men of God with loving and caring hearts.

My daughters-in-love, Latoya and Candice, for loving God, loving their husbands, and accepting me as a mom.

My siblings and their families. My brother, Aubrey, and his wife, Lucy. My sister, Marcia, and her husband, Hubert. My nephews, Isaac, Austin, Eric, and Travis. Thank you for your love, prayers, support, and for always being there for me.

My friends who have blessed me with their love, laughter, and genuine friendship.

My prayer partners, whose intercessions over the years for myself and my family have been invaluable.

My church family and all the churches and pastors, who have allowed me to minister to their congregations in whatever capacity over the years.

The many Daughters of Destiny, who have allowed me to speak into their lives and encourage them to trust in the Lord with all of their hearts.

Introduction

Have you been wounded? If you have lived life at all, of course you have. But is there purpose for the wounds? This book seeks to explore that question and reveal that there is indeed purpose for the pain. In writing this book, I seek not to do harm to any parties involved but to share my story with you, my reader, in the hope that the experiences God has taken me through will let you know that He is real, that He has a perfect plan and purpose for your life, and that He cares about you and loves you very much.

I know you may carry hurts from childhood and endure more emotional wounds and hurts just living life. This book can be used as a guide to lead you to come up higher and see your life from God's perspective as He reveals the purpose for your pain. I seek to bring healing to you by exposing my wounds and revealing how God has healed me. If God brought you to it, He can and will bring you through it. It is my life's desire to bring healing into the lives of wounded people, whether they have been wounded through past hurts, toxic relationships, disappointments, or rejections. I desire to tell them that they don't have to live life in misery with anger, bitterness, or hate.

I have long believed that it is time for Christians to take

the masks off and stop pretending that their lives are perfect or that they have never experienced problems since they received Christ. It is time for Christians to be real with themselves, their God, and others. I also want unbelievers to know that life is so much more than the wounds they receive, whether the wounds are emotional, mental, physical, spiritual, or even financial; life is about getting to know the God of Abraham, Isaac, and Jacob, who seeks a real relationship with them. I want you, reader, to meet a Savior called Jesus of Nazareth, the Christ, who understands ridicule, betrayal, judgment, and humiliation. He understands, not just because He is God but also because He became flesh and walked the life of a human man. He understands because of direct experience. I can think of no greater humiliation than being stripped naked, nailed by your hands and feet to a wooden pole, and lifted up in front of your family, friends, and enemies for all to see your slow and agonizing death, having been falsely accused and mistaken for a common criminal. We can never say God doesn't know what we're going through because that would not be the truth.

And so, I share a small part of my journey of being wounded and healed in the hopes that my wounds will help someone else to know that God is good all the time. Whichever way you have been wounded, the wounds serve a purpose if you allow them to. God works all things together for good to those who love Him, to those who are called according to His purpose. Trust this God to heal, deliver, and redeem you as He has me.

At the end of each chapter is an application. The truths

you learn will do you little good if you do not apply them to your own situation and life. The application allows you to do something tangible, to show you understand the concept and that you are willing to make a positive change in your life.

After the application is a prayer for God to intervene in your situation. Take a moment to read the prayer and make it your own. I encourage you to be as specific as you can in your prayers. After all, you are talking to the One—the only One who can change things in your life and bring you wholeness and healing. It is my prayer that this book will bring healing to your wounded soul as you commit and recommit your life to Christ. Shalom.

Chapter One

Surrender to God

"And Mary said, Behold the handmaid of the Lord;
be it unto me according to they word..."
Luke 1:38 (KJV)

The Handmaiden of the Lord

What happens when you surrender your life to God, and He leads you into a difficult situation? Has God ever given you clear direction to do something, you do it, and then it turns out not as you imagined? Perhaps you might even say it turned out wrong? This would make you wonder if you heard from God in the first place and say, "Lord, how could You tell me to do something, I follow Your directions, and then it turns out wrong?" This was my question to God concerning my marriage. God led me to marry my husband, but things went wrong from the beginning. Finally, after thirty years together, our marriage collapsed in failure. Did I make a mistake? Had I really heard from God? And, if so, why did God allow me to go through what I did?

Everyone, whether they will admit it or not, would like to get married at some point in their life. But what does that mean? It means that they want to find "the one" or the person they love and who loves them. They want to share their life with someone around whom they can genuinely be themselves, who gets their jokes and enjoys spending time with them. They desire someone they can build a happy and productive life with. Everyone is in pursuit of happiness. However, I believe that pursuing happiness means surrendering to God and asking Him what His plans are for your life. You can only be truly happy when you discover your life's purpose.

And so, even though I did want to be married, I surrendered my life to the Lord and trusted in His sovereignty as to whether I was to marry or not. I prayed to God saying: *Behold, the handmaid of the Lord. Be it unto me according to Your Word.* I knew Mary uttered these words when the angel Gabriel told her she would conceive the Christ Child without a man being involved (Luke 1: 38). I'm sure this must have been an incredibly difficult sentence for her to say because, in surrendering her life to God, she was placed in a challenging situation. Mary had to face rejection from her family, her community, and even her own fiancé. But throughout all of it, God was with her. So, I prayed to be God's handmaid and surrendered my singlehood to Him. It was difficult, but I truly meant it. I made this decision after listening to a taped sermon by a pastor who was talking to singles. The pastor asked for singles not to be caught up in seeking out a mate but rather to surrender the whole process to the Lord. He said to surrender it and give up any preconceived ideas imposed by the world or the church concerning a person's right to get married. You, as a believer who has asked Jesus to come into your heart, are now a new creation in Christ Jesus. You are not under any mandates of the world or the church to do or live life according to their view of what your life should look like.

One of these views is marriage. What if you never marry? What if that is not God's perfect will for your life in this earthly realm? Would you be okay with it? Do you love God enough to allow Him to choose for you if He does want you to marry? Do you trust Him enough to really surrender your life into His Hands? The message struck a chord with me. Did I have a right to be married? Who had given me this right? The Bible says that those who receive Him have a right to become the children of God (John 1:12). It didn't say that they have a right to be married. In fact, the Apostle Paul says that if you are married when you receive the Lord, you shouldn't seek to divorce. Conversely, he says that if you are single when you receive the Lord, you shouldn't seck to marry (1 Corinthians 7:8). The Apostle Paul implies that we are to have a singular devotion to the Lord. In fact, this state is best for us because it comes with less trouble. He does say, of course, that it would be better to marry than to burn. I assume that he means to burn with lust for another individual as in a marriage. In any event, being married is not a God-given right.

21

Marriage is an assumption in our society, and pressure is put on singles, even by the church, to find their Boaz or Ruth. This pressure is undue and not of God. No one should feel pressured to do anything. The churches that I knew and the church folks that I was around made it seem like there was something wrong with you as a single person if you were not married in your twenties. Some even implied that you should be looking for your other or better half. If this is true, then it equally implies that you are one half of a person—not a whole one. I found objection to that because God, through Christ, has made us whole. In fact, it says in Genesis 2:24 that the two become one. There is no real miracle in one half and one half becoming one; the miracle is in two becoming one—one whole plus one whole equaling one.

In any event, I was pressured to date and get married. Well-meaning friends even set me up on blind dates, but none of them went well. God then told me that the purpose of dating was not to have something to do on a Saturday night. He wanted His people to enter into courtship rather than date. Courtship says, "I am looking at you as more than a way to conquer loneliness on a Friday or Saturday night. I'm looking at you as a potential mate, a potential spouse." Dating is like trying on shoes in a shoe store and wearing them for a short while, then kicking them off and going on to the next pair. Courtship is taking the time to get to know the shoes, get a feel for them, walk in them for a while, then make the decision that they are worth purchasing. You commit and say, "I love you, and now I'm going to invest in making you mine. You are special to me." I decided to trust God and be His handmaid, whatever that entailed. If I never got married, so be it, and if He led me to someone He wanted me to marry, so be it. As long as I was in the perfect will of God, I believed I would be fine. So, I surrendered my life to His will.

Application

Do you know that you are special to God? He formed you in your mother's womb, and He wants you to have a right relationship with Him. God wants you to surrender to Him. God wants to be Lord in every area of your life, especially in something as big as whom you should marry or if you should marry at all.

It first begins with you repenting of going your own way. Instead, ask Jesus to come into your heart to be your Savior. Ask Him to be your Lord as well. This means, He is now in control of your life. He is in the driver's seat, and you willingly submit to a loving God who only wants the best for you. Jeremiah 29:11 says: "'For I know the plans I have for you,' declares the LORD, 'plans to prosper you and not to harm you, plans to give you hope and a future'" (NIV). If you trust Him to be Lord of your life, whatever you do will be in alignment with the perfect will of God.

Take a minute right now and tell God that you surrender to Him. Tell Him that you believe Jesus took the penalty for your sins and disobedience, which was death, and that He died on the cross in your place. Tell Him that you believe Jesus rose again from the dead, is living today, and is ready and able to make you a new creature. Tell God that you surrender your will to His. Not your will, but His be done. Ask Him also to help you live that out. Watch what great things God will do with little when it is placed in His Hands. It is safe to surrender your life to God. Follow Him as He leads you. His promise is never to leave you or forsake you (Hebrews 13:5); you will not be put to shame when you trust the Lord (Psalm 25:1-3).

Always remember, without Christ, you cannot do anything. But with Him, you can do all things, for He will give you strength (Philippians 4:13). Jesus being Lord of your life means you accept Him as King over your life; He has free reign in your life. It means that you are done going your own way, messing up, falling down, and stumbling around in the dark not knowing where you are going. It means Jesus is now a lamp unto your feet and a light unto your path (Psalms 119:105). It means you have a wonderful life before you. And so, the journey begins.

Prayer:

Dear Lord Jesus,

I repent of going my own way and not surrendering my life to You. I know that You are good and that the plans You have for me are also good. I surrender my life fully to You now. I ask You, Lord, to come into my heart and make me a new creation. Teach me how to live a surrendered life and use me for Your honor and Your glory. Amen.

Chapter Two

Pray About Everything

"Be anxious for nothing, but in everything by prayer and supplication, with thanksgiving, let your requests be made known to God."
Philippians 4:6

Courtship & Wedding

It is safe to pray about everything. Philippians 4:6 reminds us not to be anxious about anything but instead to pray about everything. As a Christian, I prayed about everything in my life. I wanted God to take priority and be first in my life— so much so that I had given up my "right" to be married as a young woman in my late twenties. Based on my reading of Luke 1:38, I simply told the Lord: *Behold the handmaid of the*

Lord, be it unto me according to Your will. Then, I left it there. I would be fine, whether He wanted me to marry or not. In either case, I would serve Him with my life. I surrendered all to the Lord, unlike many of my peers, who, at the time, were obsessed with finding their Boaz.

I found that many women and men also attended churches with large congregations just to scout out for a mate and see who was available. I was a member of one such church before I met my husband, but I was not there to scout out the land. I was an active member of the church and participated whenever the church doors were open. One Sunday, after a particularly anointed service where the Lord spoke and tears ran down my face in response to the power of being in His presence, a female acquaintance saw me and approached me on the way out. She did not ask, "How did you enjoy the service?" or, "Wow, wasn't that service so awesome?" Instead, lifting the ring finger of her left hand, she asked me, "Anything yet?" By this question, she meant to ask if I had found my Boaz and gotten engaged yet. Ending such an anointed service by asking if I "had met Mr. Right" indicated a deep spiritual problem. I simply said, "No," and kept on moving.

On another occasion, I was invited to a friend's house for fellowship. I do not remember us praying at any point, but I do remember that she showed me something extraordinary: she had a trunk in her bedroom with her wedding dress and her trousseau. Was she engaged? No. Was she even in a serious dating relationship? No. She had the trousseau ready for when the time came. I do not believe the time ever came for her. I had no trousseau or wedding dress, and I was not sulking around waiting for my Boaz. I told her that I had given up my right to be married, and I never went back to her apartment. Shortly after, I met my future husband. To say I was not looking was an understatement.

My husband and I were introduced to each other through a mutual friend and, yes, at that same large church. I prayed over our relationship from the start. I never gave him my phone number. He gave me his and invited me to call him. After I asked God in prayer if I should call or not, the Lord led me to make that phone call, which led to nightly phone conversations. God knew that the only man I would ever entertain for marriage or even date had to be born again. He had to have a relationship with the Lord and not just attend Sunday services; he had to be a true man of God.

It was God who made it clear to both of us that we were to be husband and wife. Every time I asked God for confirmation whether I should marry this man, He gave it to me. He used conventional ways, such as preached sermons or Bible studies, and unconventional ways, such as being approached by absolute strangers who remarked that we made a lovely couple.

The wedding and wedding plans were also surrendered into God's Hands. I even asked God what date He wanted us to marry, and He gave me a date in December of that same year. Now, you know this had to be God because it never entered my mind to be married in a winter month especially not so close to Christmas. God told me the exact date of the wedding, which, when I checked the calendar, was on a Saturday. It was the only feasible date at that time for my wedding. Before my husband and I were even engaged, I witnessed a wedding at the church I was attending. God spoke to me and said, "Around this time next year." I instantly understood that to mean that I would be getting married around that time the following year. That wedding was at 3:00 p.m., and my actual wedding was exactly 365 days later at 5:00 p.m. I had forgotten this experience until God gave me my wedding date and reminded me of what He had previously said.

I also asked God what wedding ceremony He would like conducted. I was led to a little booklet called *A Ceremony of Marriage* by Kenneth Copeland. I never knew it existed. The pastor who married us told us that he would do the wedding, but the only wedding ceremony he would do was—yes, you already know it—*A Ceremony of Marriage* by Kenneth Copeland! I told the pastor, "No problem."

I was thirty-one years old—an "old maid" by the world's standards—when I got married. The wedding ceremony was a bit unusual, to say the least. The presence of God was strong in the sanctuary, and prophetic words came forth during the ceremony. God encouraged us prophetically through the pastor, and then a wedding attendee stood up, spoke in tongues, and gave the interpretation. It was a prophetic word to the congregation who witnessed the ceremony, charging them to pray for us and not to tamper with what God had joined together. We would really need those prayers.

Application

Do you pray? Do you pray only about the big things or only when you feel that you need God's immediate help in a situation? Is prayer a lifestyle for you? It should be, especially if you are a believer. We should pray about the decisions in life that we must make—decisions that affect our quality of life. If we make bad decisions, there are consequences that must be faced. If we make good decisions, not only is our life better for it, but the lives of the people around us and those we love and care for, are better for it as well. That's why you must pray before making major decisions in your life. Life will be so much easier as you pray about everything. It doesn't mean that everything will be perfect, but it does mean that you can hear from God; He will direct your path. No matter if your path leads you into a pit or a palace, God is with you. He wants to shape and mold your character. He wants to conform your will to His. Let Him.

So, how do you pray? Psalm 100:4 says, "Enter into His gates with thanksgiving, and into His courts with praise." Prayer is simply talking to your Heavenly Father. We have access to God the Father through Christ Jesus the Son by the Holy Spirit. When you approach God in prayer, begin by praising Him and recognizing that He is God. Thank Him for His goodness and faithfulness. Philippians 4:6 says to make your requests known to God, and Matthew 7:7 says to ask and you will receive. You do not have to use superficial, flowery "church" language to pray. Speak as you would to a friend or confidant. Speak from your heart. And please, if the Holy Spirit brings to your mind something that you did that displeased the Father, acknowledge it and repent of it. Apologize to God! Say you're sorry, and ask Him to help you not commit that sin again. When you pray, try to be as honest, real, and as transparent as you can. Ask in the authority of the Name of Jesus given to every believer.

After you speak, sit quietly, and listen for God's response to you. It may come as a still small voice (1 Kings 19:11-12), or it may be a scripture that leaps off the page to you; it may be a "knowing in your knower" (a powerful sense of something that you receive). Regardless, He will respond. Write down in a journal what you believe God is saying to you. This will strengthen your faith as you reread it in times of difficulty. Don't rush your prayer time. Set aside a time each day to spend praying and listening to God's voice. Ask Him to use you in His service. It is the highest honor to be a servant of the Living God. A man of God once shared with me that God has chosen us because He loves us, and He has allowed us to remain joyful even in the midst of suffering. I believe this joy comes from having a strong prayer life.

Prayer:

Dear Lord,
I have decided to follow You. I choose to make prayer a priority and part of my lifestyle. I choose to pray about every decision I make and not to be anxious about my life. As I acknowledge

You, thank You for leading and guiding me on the path You have chosen for me. Amen.

Chapter Three

God's Pruning

". . . every branch that bears fruit He prunes, that it
may bear more fruit."
John 15:2

Cut by God

The courtship, the wedding, the marriage ceremony, and the marriage itself were all bathed in prayer from the get-go. So, what went wrong? I don't see it anymore in terms of what went wrong. Instead, I choose to believe that I needed to go through what I did. There was a purpose in my wounds. There are wounds, and then there are wounds. I learned over the years that the wounds were never meant to destroy me; God allowed me to experience them so that I could bear fruit, more fruit, and much fruit. I have learned to abide in my Lord and Savior Jesus Christ. John 15:5 speaks of abiding. It uses the grapevine as a metaphor for abiding in a relationship with Jesus Christ. Jesus is the vine, and those who are in union with Him—connected to Him—are the branches. I must abide in the vine because I cannot bear fruit apart from the vine.

In describing the state of a branch on the grapevine, Jesus tells us in John 15 that the branches on a grapevine must be cut, or wounded, through a process called pruning. To eliminate dead or diseased parts of the plant, as well as reshape them, grapevines must be trimmed as soon as they start growing; they continue to be pruned as the plant branches out and matures. Vines left to grow on their own may not necessarily develop sweet and juicy grapes, but deliberate pruning of the branches on the vine will indeed produce the good quality fruit the vinedresser wants. A select pruning process is essential for the vine to continue to produce quality fruit each year. Grapevines left unpruned can easily grow into unmanageable tangles, resulting in decreased fruit production.

As grapevine branches must be pruned, so must believers (as branches connected to Jesus, the vine) be pruned by a loving vinedresser, our Heavenly Father. Pruning cuts off all unproductive parts: branches that are unlike God, branches growing in the wrong direction, and wild branches. The purpose of cutting is not to hurt, but it is to help the branch grow in the right direction and ultimately bear good fruit. Branches that are productive and bear good fruit must also be pruned so that they will bear even more fruit.

When Christians are pruned, many of them tend to misunderstand or misinterpret God's actions. Imagine the bewilderment of a grapevine when the farmer must cut and prune its branches. But the good farmer knows that the cut, no matter how painful, has purpose and will yield a good result. The vine is a symbol for God's providential care and steadfast love toward His people, and we, the people, are the branches. Jesus is the vine from whom we draw strength and nourishment. God the Father is the vinedresser; He is a good farmer, and He strategically cuts. He takes care of the vineyard, but believers tend to question God when they are cut. They think, *Why is this cut happening to me? Lord, why have you forsaken me? Lord, don't you care? Don't you see? Don't you love me, Lord?* It is not because God does not love you or that He does not care that He prunes you; it is not that you did or are doing something wrong. It is because you are doing something right. It is because you are bearing fruit. It is all for the glory of God. 1 Peter 4:12-13 reads:

> Friends, when life gets really difficult, don't jump to the conclusion that God isn't on the job. Instead, be glad that you are in the very thick of what Christ experienced. This is a spiritual refining process, with glory just around the corner. (The Message)

No disciplined life goes without being cut, but where the cut is, faith grows. Growth and bearing fruit depend on your perspective of the cut. You must see the cut as coming from a loving God who needs to prune you, not from an angry, disapproving God who hates you. He prunes you so that your life can be productive and so that you can bear fruit. Fruit of a good character and fruit of the spirit: love, joy, peace, goodness, meekness, kindness, longsuffering, and self-control. You can bear fruit that others can see, taste, and eat to satisfy their souls.

Jesus was cut. Isaiah 53:5 says that He was wounded for our transgressions and bruised for our iniquities. His cuts were for a purpose. How can anyone truly follow in His footsteps without being cut? You are cut when you endure the pain of the death of a loved one, a child, a spouse, a mom, or a dad. You are cut when you lose a successful job. You are cut when your dream house is foreclosed on or burned to the ground. You are cut when you receive an unfavorable doctor's report. You are cut when you survive a toxic or abusive relationship. You are, cut in the death of a marriage through separation or divorce. That was how I was cut. That is how I was wounded. The failure of my marriage was a deep wound because, without any doubt, I knew that it was ordained by God. So, how could it come to an end? That's a fair question and one that I have asked the Lord, myself.

Since I had given up my right to be married, it came as a surprise to me to meet the man who was to be my husband shortly after. We were married about a year and a half after we met. I know that God wanted me to marry this person, and I strongly believe that my marriage was part of my purpose and destiny. It was an assignment that the Lord had given me. No, it was not a cold, hard assignment. There was definitely love, and we had many good times before we were married. But my assignment was to grow up in the Lord by being cut to bear fruit, more fruit, and much fruit.

My faith was tested and tried. I have no regrets being

married, and everything that has happened in my marriage has truly brought me to where I am today. I am ministering today from a point of view of experience and wisdom instead of anger or bitterness. I have learned many life lessons, including the biggest one anyone could learn, which is that I learned about myself. I also learned to have faith in God, what it truly means to trust Him with all my heart, and not to lean unto my own understanding. I learned, if I acknowledged Him in all my ways, that He would direct my path (Proverbs 3:5-6).

I learned about myself and about my relationship with the Lord. I also learned life lessons, such as how to deal with difficult people. I learned that a wise woman builds her house, and the foolish tears it down with her own hands (Proverbs 14:1). I learned patience, tact, and how to pray. I also had an assignment to bring into the earthly realm—two amazing human beings—when I gave birth to my sons. God's perfect will is in decency and order. His plan for my marriage included giving birth. He did not want this done outside of my marital relationship.

The wounds that I suffered in my marriage were used by God to prune and position me. Growth cannot occur apart from cuts. I was wounded through my husband's many indiscretions with women. I was wounded because of emotional, mental, spiritual, and financial abuses. Through it all, though, I learned to trust in Jesus. The song writer, Andre Crouch, reminds us in a song that problems allow us to find out what God can do in our lives. Now, don't misunderstand me. Yes, I cried many a season until I had no more tears to shed. I felt like the psalmist

King David, when he wrote that he cried so long and hard that he made his bed to swim (Psalm 6:6). I cried and cried out to God, and it is He who gave me the strength to not only survive, but to thrive after what I had suffered. The fact that I can minister to women today is because I understand the pain of rejection and betrayal. I know what it's like to be manipulated and controlled by someone you love and still fight for your marriage and pull down strongholds, knowing you are not fighting flesh and blood.

Application

Are you fruitful for the Lord? Do you want to bear fruit? The branch cannot bear fruit apart from the vine. The branch must be cut and pruned to enable it to be fruit-bearing. Allow God to prune you. His cuts are precise and designed to enable you to grow, not to destroy you. Trust Him as He prunes your life. No matter how deep the cuts of rejection, betrayal, disappointment, lies, manipulation, and control are, trust God's plan. Stay connected to the vine. Bear fruit.

How can you be fruitful? Live a consistent Christian life. Read the Word of God and study the Bible each day. Use a translation that you understand. Yes, you can read the Bible on your phone or computer, but invest in a hard copy in which you can mark in the margins and highlight scriptures that are meaningful to you. Hide the Word in your heart by memorizing specific scriptures; this will be a source of encouragement to you as the Holy Spirit brings these scriptures back to your remembrance in times of trouble or struggle. Spend quality time alone with the Lord in prayer. Attend a Bible-believing church, where God's truths are not only taught but modeled. Participate in church activities and serve wherever you best fit in. Associate with other Christians who also desire to bear fruit. Challenge and encourage each other to stay vitally connected to the vine.

Prayer:

Dear Lord,

Forgive me for complaining about the necessary cuts that You must make in my life for me to be fruitful. I trust You know exactly where, how, and when to prune me. I know that I cannot bear fruit apart from You, so help me stay connected to the vine—connected to You. Thank You for Your love. Amen.

Chapter Four

* · ━━━ ◦❖◦ ━━━ · *

Bearing Fruit

*"The Spirit of the Lord God is upon Me, Because
the Lord has anointed Me . . . to heal the
brokenhearted"*
Isaiah 61:1

The Anointing of God

Each and every time I was cut, the anointing of God
would seep out of me like sap from a tree. It was evident that
God's Hand was upon me, even evident to my husband as he
planned and conducted my pastoral ordination service. Yet, the
cuts continued. They were not pleasant, I assure you, but I was
destined to bear fruit, more fruit, and much fruit. God allowed
me to teach and preach His Word and prophesy with clarity,
precision, and accuracy in the midst of the pain. No one knew

the cost of the oil in my alabaster box, but if I helped even one person along my way, it was worth it all.

When I accepted the Lord as my Savior, I was told that there was more; I could be baptized in the Holy Spirit with the evidence of speaking in tongues. I hungered for this experience. Years before I met my husband, I attended a conference conducted by Evangelist Oral Roberts at his university in Tulsa, Oklahoma. At the conference, I bought every book and workbook on the Holy Spirit. There was even a special night dedicated to receiving the Holy Spirit. I attended, asking God in faith to baptize me in the Holy Spirit. I opened my mouth, but nothing came out. I left the conference disappointed, but I had purchased Oral Roberts' booklet, *If You Want to Receive the Holy Spirit With the Evidence of Speaking in Tongues, Do These Things*.

When I came home from the conference, at the first chance I could, I locked myself in the bathroom, which was my private prayer closet. In my hand, I had the little booklet. I was determined to do the things that the booklet talked about and receive the infilling of the Holy Spirit. First, the booklet said to receive Jesus as Lord and Savior, which I had already done. Second, the booklet instructed the reader to ask the Father for this gift based on Luke 11:13, which says, "If you then, being evil, know how to give good gifts to your children, how much more will your heavenly Father give the Holy Spirit to those who ask Him!" I asked, but, as I read the booklet, something occurred to me that I had never thought of before. I was literally waiting for the Holy Spirit to take over my tongue and make me speak in another language. The booklet said that this is not the way in which it will happen. The Holy Spirit is a gentleman and will not force anyone to do anything. Rather, I was to yield my voice and mouth to the Holy Spirit.

I read that I was supposed to just open my mouth and begin to praise God out loud. As I began to do this, in only a few minutes, I felt a bubbling up from my stomach. I yielded my tongue, and out of my mouth I heard words coming out that I had never heard before. I could hardly believe that it was me speaking, but it was. I spoke in tongues for ten or fifteen minutes. From the booklet, I also learned to ask God for the interpretation so that I could pray in English after I spoke in tongues. When we are speaking in tongues, we are speaking directly to God, and, even though our spirit is edified, our mind does not know what is being said. Therefore, after you speak in tongues or your heavenly prayer language, ask God for the interpretation. It will not be a word-for-word translation, but He will give you the gist of what was spoken. I did that and began asking the Holy Spirit to pray through me. I would often begin a prayer in tongues, then transition to praying in English. From there, as the Lord led, I would go back to tongues and give a prophecy, a word God spoke into my spirit.

As I asked the Holy Spirit to pray through me, I would hear what the next words would be and often my prayers would transition to prophecy: "Thus saith the Spirit of the Living God." I could feel the anointing of God as I prayed. The people in our church saw and felt this anointing, and my husband even saw it, which is the reason why he ordained me as a pastor. I was already preaching, teaching, and conducting Sunday school in my church, as well as leading praise and worship often. The next logical step was for me to be ordained. I remember at the time that my husband and I were friends with a certain pastor and his wife. This pastor told me that, if my husband was not going to ordain me as a pastor, he would. I am thankful that my husband saw the anointing on my life and was obedient to God to ordain me. I was bearing fruit, but more fruit was to come.

Application

Are you born again? Have you been baptized in the Holy Spirit since you believed? Have you received the Holy Spirit with the evidence of speaking in tongues? Some might argue that there is no such thing as speaking in tongues, but the Apostle Paul found believers who had not even heard of the Holy Spirit. After correct instruction by Him, they were indeed baptized in the Holy Spirit with the evidence of speaking in tongues (Acts 19:1-7). Further, some might argue that speaking in tongues was only possible during the time period in which the first disciples lived. Yet, millions of Christians, including myself, speak in tongues today. First Corinthians 12:10 says that tongues and the interpretation of tongues are gifts of the Spirit.

Some might argue that we don't need to speak in tongues to be saved. Although this is true, as a believer, wouldn't you want all that Christ Jesus died to give you? He said that He would not leave us as orphans, and the Holy Spirit would come to be our teacher, guide, and helper. Jesus said to ask that our joy may be full (John 15:11). It is an amazing joy to speak in tongues, knowing that your loving Heavenly Father is hearing you and that you are in vital communication with Him. I predominantly use tongues as my prayer language as I still pray in the spirit, and then I pray with the understanding in English. I challenge you to ask God for this amazing gift and to not be afraid of all God wants you to experience.

God wants you to experience the power of the Holy Spirit, referred to as the anointing of God. In the Bible, oil, especially olive oil, was used to anoint priests, prophets, kings, and anyone God wanted to use. Oil represented His presence, authority, and power in their lives.

The process by which olive oil is produced gives us a clear picture of what happens in the life of a believer during times of adversity. The olives must be crushed, pressed, and squeezed for oil to be produced. So it is with our lives: as we are pressed from all sides, crushed but not in despair, we find that God's anointing is poured out upon us. He has promised to never leave or forsake us. In fact, in the times of my most severe adversity and trials, I found that God's presence was with me all the more. He spoke through me into the lives of others to enlighten and encourage them. He gave me a compassionate heart toward others, and He allowed me to come up higher and see my life from His perspective. I challenge you not to run from the pressing and crushing of adversity but to trust God and allow Him to anoint you with fresh oil. He will strengthen you, as well as enable you to minister to others—not in your own ability, but in His.

Prayer:

Dear Heavenly Father,
I recognize that You give good gifts. I desire all that Jesus died to make available to me. I ask for the anointing of the Holy Spirit in my life. I seek You now for the baptism of the Holy Spirit with the evidence of speaking in tongues. As I praise You, I yield my tongue to the Holy Spirit and thank You for the gifts of speaking in tongues and the interpretation of tongues. I will pray in the Spirit and with my understanding. Amen.

Chapter Five

The Purposes of God

"He Himself gave some to be apostles, some prophets, some evangelists, and some pastors and teachers, for the equipping of the saints for the work of ministry, for the edifying of the body of Christ."
Ephesians 4:11-12

Pastor/Teacher/Wife/Mother

I knew, when God revealed to me that I was going to be married, that I would marry a minister. I knew that I was to be a minister's wife. One of the confirming scriptures God gave me was 1 Corinthians 7:2: ". . . let every man have his own wife, and let every woman have her own husband" (KJV). Another confirmation came one day while I was reading a book by Evelyn Christenson entitled *Lord, Change Me*. She shared her experience about marrying a minister. Her first name was Evelyn and my maiden name was Evelyn (pronounced Eve–lyn). When I read what she wrote on the page about God calling her "Evelyn" and telling her she was to be a minister's wife, the words leapt off the page to me. It felt like I was hit in the stomach. I felt the presence of God, and it was a knowing in my knower. I knew that God was speaking to me. I, too, would marry a minister.

My fiancé was already doing the work of an evangelist, and although he wanted to be a pastor, He was not yet ordained. However, he was a natural evangelist. By this, I mean that he carried around a big Bible and concordance, a notebook, and a pen everywhere he went, even on his commutes on the train. He told me at the time that he never knew where or when God would speak to him, so he wanted to be prepared. And prepared he was.

He would strike up conversations with strangers on the train, and the dialogue would always go to the status of their salvation. I witnessed this many times when we traveled together on the train. I admired his boldness to speak and the clarity with which he spoke. The conversations were all about people's perceptions of Jesus. He told me years later, as I was being prepared for ordination, to always hand the Bible to the person to whom I was witnessing and allow them to read the Bible passage for themselves. For example, I shouldn't simply quote Romans 10:9-10, but I should have the person read it out loud. Then, that person will see that the words are not mine but that they are written in the Bible. As they read the Word, God would speak to them.

My fiancé also prayed for folks after he witnessed to them. He would ask if they wanted to receive Jesus as their personal Lord and Savior, then lead them to Christ right where they were. I've seen him do it on the train, in the streets, and even in a bank one time. He also told me to leave my eyes open while I prayed in public places just to be aware of my surroundings.

Although I believed that I would marry a minister, I truly had no idea that God was calling me to be ordained as well. Quite frankly, I was content at that time with my role as a minister's wife. Later, as my husband was ordained as a pastor, I was fine being a pastor's wife. I understood that the mantle of pastor was not something to take lightly. I did not desire this mantle, and I did not seek it out or choose it for myself. But living a life of obedience to God is often full of surprises around every turn on the journey of life. If I refused to be ordained, I would have been walking in false humility, which is the flip side of pride.

Did I not trust God enough to walk in my purpose and destiny? Was I looking at only my limited abilities, or was I looking at the Lord God Almighty, in whom there is no variableness or shadow of turning in His decisions? I prayed, fasted, sought godly counsel, and waited on God to bring confirmation that this was indeed what He wanted for my life. Fueled with God's confirmation and reassurance, I accepted the assignment of being ordained as a pastor.

So, in this season of life, I was now an ordained pastor, school teacher, a wife, and a mother of two young children. I was walking in some very big jobs and responsibilities.

Application

Has God called you to do something, but you are afraid to do it? Are you afraid to say "yes" to God? Remember that God has not given you a spirit of fear but of power, love, and a sound mind (2 Timothy 1:7). If God brought you to it, He Himself will lead you through it. He will never give you more than you are able to bear. He may even have you make a course adjustment if you're becoming overwhelmed with an assignment. Fast, pray, and ask God for confirmation as to what He wants you to do, then do it. Do it even if you do it afraid. Just do it.

Prayer:

Dear Lord,
Thank You for the purposes You have for my life. I ask now for the courage to do what You have called me to do. I know that You are the strength of my life, and I do not walk alone because You are always with me. I pray to accept and complete every assignment You give to me. May my life bring glory to Your Name. Amen.

Chapter Six

Walk in Faith

"Now faith is the substance of things hoped for, the
evidence of things not seen."
Hebrew 11:1

Trusting God in Everything

Sickness

I had many major responsibilities as a pastor, schoolteacher, wife, and mother, and I was tired all the time. I attributed my exhaustion to the fact that I wore so many hats. As a mother of two young children, I was responsible to get them ready for school. They were fed and dressed, then we traveled by train to their school. From there, I took a bus to work, where I engaged in a full day of teaching highly active second graders. After I left work, I did everything in reverse: I took the bus or walked to my children's school to pick them up, traveled home on the train, and often stopped at the grocery store to buy food for dinner. Then, I cooked dinner, fed the children, and made sure they completed their homework.

As pastors, my husband and I held church services in our home. Friday was prayer meeting night, so we had to transform our living room to receive the congregation. We set up microphones, had sound checks, and set up the podium and chairs. I ministered and prayed with everyone. Sunday came, and our home had to be set up again for service. Service programs were prepared, worship was led, and all the kids, including my own, were taken to a bedroom where I conducted children's church. Not to mention, I also graded papers on the weekend, did lesson plans for the upcoming school week, and (once in a while) actually talked with my husband. This was all outside of special events and activities at home, my children's school, work, or with my family.

I was tired, so tired that I never saw my hands shaking one day at work while I was writing a note. I was in the school office writing a message, and a colleague pointed it out to me. She encouraged me to see a doctor and have it checked out. It was early October, and a new school term had just started. I hardly had enough time to do lesson plans, grade papers, and get my classroom decorated and organized on top of providing for my family's and church family's needs, let alone time for myself. However, everything changed on Columbus Day in October 1994.

My husband and I had an argument after church, of course. He didn't want me to accompany him to the hospital to visit a very sick church member. She requested to be water baptized, so we wanted to honor that request before she passed into the arms of the Lord. The baptism was modified since she could not leave her hospital bed. I assumed that we would go together, so I made plans for the church secretary, who occasionally babysat for us, to watch the children. Monday was the Columbus Day holiday, so my sons were off from school and so was I. However, my husband didn't want me to accompany him to the hospital and was upset that I had made arrangements with the church secretary without discussing it with him first. The argument ended badly, and I was left crying and visibly shaken.

He went to the hospital alone, and I stayed home to try to catch up on grading papers before the holiday was over. The next day, when I woke up, my hand was not the only thing that was shaking. My entire body was shaking from head to foot. I felt the shaking deep within me. As there was no one to take my kids to school, I took a train ride with them to school. I then returned home, got myself together, and went to my doctor's office. I distinctly remember my husband yelling to me out of the window as I walked away saying, "Whose gonna pick up the kids?" I hadn't thought that far ahead, apparently. I was already upset that he didn't go with me to the doctor. At the very least, since he wasn't working, he was entirely capable of picking up the kids from school. In any event, I went to the doctor to find out the cause of my shaking. I went alone, but I trusted God all the way.

The wait to see the doctor was very long. When I was

finally called in to see him, he examined me and told me that I had Graves' disease. Graves' disease is an autoimmune disease that causes your thyroid to become overactive and produce more thyroid hormone than the body needs. Also referred to as hyperthyroidism, Graves' causes your body's metabolism, including your heart rate, to speed up. In my case, the disease was directly linked to my mental, emotional, and physical stress.

The news came as a surprise to me, as I had never heard of Graves' disease before. I had been ignoring physical symptoms for a long time, and, in taking care of others, I neglected to take care of myself. Of course, as a Christian, I prayed to God for healing, but I wound up in a hospital. It was there that God told me that He put me in the hospital to rest. Yes, I was there to get treated for my ailment, but I was also there to rest. I was on the verge of burnout, fatigue, and total exhaustion. It is sad when your life is so stressful that the best place for you is in a hospital bed, but I was able to rest in the hospital and receive care for my stress-induced illness. While in the hospital, I learned that the world, and my world, continued and would have continued even if I were no longer in it. I thank God that He had other plans for me and allowed me to get the rest that I needed. Although I was in the hospital, my children were still fed, they still arrived at their school on time, my students were still being educated, and the church in my home continued. I left the hospital after successful treatment.

Homelessness

God had called me to rest, and that included rest from work. He told me to cut all ties with my school and resign from my teaching position. Let me stop here for a minute and say that it is important to make sure that it is God speaking to you if you decide to quit a job. I assure you this decision was bathed in prayer and not entered into lightly. When I made the decision not to go back to work, as I was led to by God, my husband was still working. However, he quit his job shortly after. Somewhere in the back of my mind, I felt like he was saying, "Well, if she won't work, neither will I."

With neither of us working, money became scarce. We were eligible for welfare because we had underage children, which was a blessing and allowed us to buy food, but food was all that we were able to afford. After about two years of being in and out of court with our landlord, we finally reached a point where we could no longer stay in our apartment due to unpaid rent. The landlord had filed a final eviction notice with the court, and the city marshal was coming. We had literal days to get out, and we did not have another apartment.

We could not afford another apartment, but we did have something lined up. I asked my dad, who owned a brownstone with rooms that he rented out, if I could move back in temporarily. This experience was both humbling and humiliating. Nevertheless, he initially agreed that our family could stay there. Moving day came. We had a friend who rented us a truck to help move our things. But the same day we were to move back in my parents' house, my dad changed his mind and said that we could not come.

I don't blame my dad at all because, looking back, I know he heard from God. I had a different destiny than to go back home. This was all part of my personal walk of faith. Nevertheless, I was devastated, but God always has a plan. A good friend of mine, who was a pastor's wife, had come to my apartment to help me pack that day. She was there when I got the news about not being able to move into my dad's house. We were all packed up without a place to go. Through tears, I asked, "God, what is going on? What do I do now?" Thankfully, this all happened in the morning while my kids were safely at school. Right away, my friend told me, "Heather, you will not be homeless." She said my family and I could stay with her and her husband. Ironically, part of their ministry was providing shelter for people who were in transition; that is, people struggling with addictions, who had recently committed their lives to the Lord and were homeless. These people had accepted Jesus as their Savior and needed to recover from alcohol and/or drug addiction. They participated in a twelve-month program in which they were immersed in the Word of God and worked on getting and staying sober while they looked for a job and a decent apartment. In other words, the program offered them discipleship and an opportunity to make a complete turnaround of their lives.

The building was three stories high, and the pastor and his wife had people in there all the time. But residents were not in the pastor and his wife's separate apartment because that was on the ground floor. It was there that my family and I were invited to stay. The apartment had two bedrooms and a pastor's office that led directly to the street. They also had two children who shared a single room with two twin beds; this was my family's bedroom for three months. God was still training, growing, and teaching me how to have faith and trust in Him.

The first night that my family arrived, Faith walked in. The pastor's wife braided hair in her home for extra money, and she had a client that first evening we came. Her name was Faith. The pastor's wife introduced me. When she said her name, I immediately heard a message from the Lord saying to have faith in Him. As Faith walked in, so faith in God must walk into my life. It was not over; all was not lost. There was yet a purpose, a higher purpose, and obviously one that I could not see. Homelessness is a major issue in any country. In the United States, thousands of people deal with it. I was blessed to have such a caring friend invite me into her modest home. Both she and her husband were good friends of my family.

As there were only two bedrooms in the small apartment, the pastor and his wife had their two children give up their bedroom so that my family could occupy it. The pastor's children moved into the bedroom that he shared with his wife. My husband and I slept on one of the twin beds, and our two sons slept on the other. All of us shared the same small bedroom. Fortunately, the boys were only six and eight at the time, so they were small enough to share. As adults, my husband and I sharing a twin-sized bed was difficult.

To tell you that this experience was the lowest of the low

does not do it justice. However, I learned that in my lowest, God is at His highest. At my worst, God is at His best. God is always leading, always speaking, and always guiding. We stayed in this home for only three months, but it was enough to give me a real heart for the homeless, the lonely, and the destitute. It was in this environment, as I prayed and asked God for my next steps, that I heard God tell me to go back to school.

Joblessness

While I was in the hospital, God clearly told me to rest. Even when I was released from the hospital, the direction was still the same: rest. I clearly heard God say to cut all ties with my job, so I resigned from my position as a teacher in October of 1994. God was faithful because He also had me draft letters to my principal, the school secretary, the staff, my colleagues, and even my students to thank them and let them know that I was starting a new chapter in my life as a full-time pastor. I left my job on excellent terms.

To say this was a walk of faith is certainly an understatement. I questioned myself, and I certainly questioned God: "What are you doing in my life?" And yet, it was during this time that I saw God's Hand and provision show up again and again. Our church had moved out of our home, and we were now renting space in the building of another ministry not too far from our apartment. With two underage children, we were eligible for food stamps, but that is not what sustained us. God's Hands literally sustained us. In fact, our church connected with other ministries, and we were able to provide a truckload of food at Thanksgiving to the church community and neighborhood. This included turkeys, burlap bags of sweet potatoes, collard greens, and dozens of pallets of dry and canned goods. In addition to that, it seemed like every time I turned around, I received a "Holy Ghost handshake." If you don't know, a Holy Ghost handshake is when someone shakes your hand and secretly passes you a love offering of paper money.

My faith was at the point where I would speak to empty cupboards and an empty refrigerator and lay hands on them in the name of Jesus. Every time, God supplied food from different sources. One day, God had me write out a grocery list of food items that I needed and wanted. Of course, I questioned God, "Why am I writing out a grocery list when I have no money to buy anything?" I was obviously still learning how to stop questioning God and just do what He says. So, in obedience and as an act of faith, I wrote out a grocery list of not only bare essentials but luxury food items. Unaware of my list and how I had prayed, my husband came home that same day with a carload of grocery bags of food! It was only through the favor of God and His supernatural provision. To my surprise and delight, my husband had bought everything on my list and more. It was just like God to do something like that. He said that He would do exceedingly and abundantly above all I could ask or think (Ephesians 4:20).

For the entire two years that I was not working, God provided naturally and supernaturally. I am humbled and thankful to say that my father, without my asking him, gave me $200 every month to help carry me through. I thanked him, of course, and he said that it was his good pleasure to give to me. This meant so much to me on many levels, but one in particular was that his words reminded me of the scripture that said it was our Heavenly Father's good pleasure to give us the kingdom (Luke 12:32). I received that financial assistance, knowing that it was not just coming from my earthly father but also from my Heavenly Father. Yet, as you may imagine, since money went to food, clothes, and utilities, there was nothing left over for rent. This lead to the eviction notice that I previously discussed.

My joblessness lasted only two years. After the Columbus Day weekend of October 1996, God led to me to return back to work as a schoolteacher. Thank God I was on good terms with everyone at my former job, especially my principal. When God told me to go back to work, I figured that, since I had left on good terms, I would go back to my same school and ask my principal to accept me as a substitute teacher. Little did I know all that God had in store.

I walked back into the school in October, a time when all the full-time teaching positions were normally already filled. My principal looked at me as I entered her office and literally exclaimed with glee: "Ms. Barfield, I'm so glad you are here! I was literally praying about a teacher to fill a recent vacancy." *What?* At that time, teachers had to take and pass the National Teachers Exam (NTE). Well, one of the last things I did before I became sick and resigned was take that exam and pass it. The teacher who was assigned to a class in the school in September had taken the exam, but she did not pass; therefore, she was not permitted to teach. My principal had to let her go. It is funny how things worked out. I remembered being upset with God at the time He asked me to leave the job. Initially, I thought, *Why did You allow me to take this three-part exam, having to pay for each part, only then to tell me to resign my teaching position?* Now, it made sense.

I also didn't know, at the time I resigned, that a teacher in good standing with the Department of Education (DOE) could resign from her position, then have two years to rescind that resignation. God is so awesome! I remember walking into my principal's office on the Tuesday right after Columbus Day; the next Monday, I was fully restored and teaching my own class. My principal had expedited all my paperwork and fingerprinting with the DOE, so I resigned from teaching in October of 1994 and was reinstated in October of 1996. I had rested for two full years from working, striving, and the daily grind of life that was sapping my life and energy. I very much needed this rest, along with an opportunity to see how God works and operates. I was learning to trust Him in all things.

Application

Without faith it is impossible to please God. Are you walking in faith today? Are you pleasing God? Hebrews 11:1 says: "Now faith is the substance of things hoped for, the evidence of things not seen." The believer's faith is not blind faith. It is believing and having knowledge of a very real God who, when you are obedient to His voice, will lead you in the path He wants you to take. We get to know His voice when we are born again. The Word says in John 10:4-5 that we know His voice, and another we will not follow. He is our Good Shepherd, and we are His sheep. He calls to us to come follow Him, and we answer.

We also get to know His voice when we read the Word of God. His Word is His voice speaking to us. Exercise your faith today. Jesus tells us that all we need is faith the size of one of the smallest seeds on earth: the mustard seed. That's all the faith we need to see God move in our lives. Mark 11:23 says that, if we have faith, we can say to any mountain to move and it will. Has God been testing your faith lately? Don't curse God and die. Trust Him and allow Him to stretch your faith. Allow Him to develop mountain-moving faith in you. Be pleasing to God today—walk in faith.

Prayer:

Dear Lord,
I exercise my faith today. I believe that You are right there with me, no matter what circumstance, trial, or temptation I am in. I trust You to stretch my faith and cause me to be pleasing in Your sight. I trust You to work all things together for my good. I choose to walk in faith. Amen.

Chapter Seven

It's Not About You

"'Not by might nor by power, but by My Spirit,'
Says the LORD of hosts."
Zechariah 4:6

Birth of Daughters of Destiny Ministry

Should I complain about my wounds when they are the very reason that I am a woman of faith today? The wounds are the reason that I have a ministry called Daughters of Destiny. It was during a difficult and painful time in my marriage that my ministry was birthed. It started as a poem. I kept a daily journal from the time I was first saved. I always signed the bottom of the blank first page of my journals as an act of surrender to God. To me, my signature meant that, however my life unfolded in the pages and however God directed my life, it was okay with me. God often spoke to me, and I wrote down what He said. He would wake me up in the middle of the night, and I would grab the pen and notebook on my nightstand and write down what He spoke into my life.

Throughout my marriage, I continued to write in my journal. Some of what I wrote were prophetic prose. One day, sitting on a park bench with tears streaming down my face, I wrote a poem called "Daughters of Destiny." I often retreated to places in nature when I wanted to be alone with the Lord. That day, my husband and I had a disagreement that left me feeling angry, emotionally drained, and disappointed. I went to my favorite park and told God that I wanted to ask for a divorce, but God once more reminded me that my life was not my own; I had surrendered it to Him. He had a purpose for my wound. It was through tears that I wrote down in my journal what God was saying to me. This is the poem that God gave me:

Daughter of Destiny

Do not give up your dreams
See them come to reality
For I, the Lord your God,
Have promised you a victorious finality.

Daughter of Destiny

Assume your Birth Position.
Push and bear down, too.
When your world is confused
And you don't know what to do.

Daughter of Destiny

Don't abort the Baby.
In the womb of your spirit
Lies a dream about to be born.
Push and bear down into it.

Daughter of Destiny

Push through the pain.
Push through the tears.
Push, I hold your hand.
Push, I know your cares.

Daughter of Destiny

It will not always be so
Trust Me – to you I give
Beauty for ashes
And the oil of joy to live.

Daughter of Destiny

I know the hurt your heart bears.
I see the tears, I know the strain
But push! It's not in vain
The Baby shall come forth through the pain.

Daughter of Destiny

My Word in you I will fulfill
Every "t" crossed,
Every "i" with a dot.
All My good Word, fail it will not.

Daughter of Destiny

As you bear down, I will comfort
As you push, I will console
Just don't abort that Baby;
Giving birth is your goal.

This poem marked the birth of the Daughters of Destiny Ministry as God led me to begin to conduct yearly women's conferences and minister to women who are brokenhearted, abused, discouraged, and disappointed in life. Being able to relate to their experiences, I have ministered to women through my own brokenness and abuse.

This ministry is still vibrant today as I continue to conduct yearly conferences. The purpose of the Daughters of Destiny Ministry is to enable, equip, and encourage women to enter into their divinely-appointed destinies.

God has consistently used me to speak life into the lives of women who have been battered or abused physically, mentally, emotionally, and spiritually. I remind women that God has not forgotten or forsaken them. I encourage them to see their trials and tribulations as part of God's perfectly divine plan; the trials and tribulations prepare them for the work He would have them do. As they learn to lean and depend on God, my goal is to assist women, much like a midwife, to give birth to their purposes and all that God has placed within the womb of their spirits.

I learned, when I surrendered my life to the Lord so many years ago, that it was no longer about me. It was no longer about what I felt that I wanted or even deserved, but it was about God and His purpose—His will being done in my life. It was about God's ability to use me to speak life into the hopeless and encourage those in despair, even those considering suicide, thinking that life had dealt them a raw deal. It was about encouraging women who were going through many challenges in life and whose marriages were in trouble or on the brink of failure. I could empathize with them. I could understand the humiliation of being homeless, being an object of ridicule and judgment, and being criticized for decisions that I've made, such as leaving a perfectly good job. I could tell them, from experience, that they will never be disappointed by putting their trust in the Lord.

God always has a plan and a purpose that is greater than we can imagine. What you may be going through right now is not just about you. If you are willing to allow God to work through you, your life can be about all the people whose lives are made better because of you.

Application

Do you think it's all about you? Do you believe God has a perfect plan for your life? We don't often see God's plan at a glance. We especially don't see it in the beginning when we are first learning to trust Him, but God is the Alpha and the Omega, the Beginning and the End. He knows the end from the beginning, and He plans accordingly. God's plan for your life is good. God is the ultimate planner and has a great plan for your life, from the cradle to the grave. As you trust God with your life, you will experience His best plan.

God says in Jeremiah 29:11, "'For I know the plans I have for you,' declares the LORD, 'plans to prosper you and not to harm you, plans to give you hope and a future'" (NIV). His best plan always comes to pass, no matter how many twists, turns, delays, and redirections we take through disobedience or plots of the enemy. Along with Jeremiah 29:11, Romans 8:28 is important to remember: ". . . all things work together for good to those who love God, to those who are called according to His purpose." God works life out for your good. God is good. Not part-time or even some of the time, but He is good all the time.

So, keep this in mind as you go through life's bumpy roads, even those that feel like rollercoasters. Hang on for the ride, never stop trusting God, and never stop believing His plan is to prosper you and give you a hope and a future. Don't get mad at God because of the things you have suffered or are suffering. Rather, spend quality time alone with Him and your Bible. Read your Bible. It is the living Word of God, and you will hear God speaking to you.

Are your trials only about you, or could they exist to help someone else? Could your life be a blessing to someone else? Could the things you've endured be used by God to encourage someone else? Second Corinthians says that God is the "God of all comfort, who comforts us in all our tribulation, that we may be able to comfort those who are in any trouble, with the comfort with which we ourselves are comforted by God" (1:3-4).

Are you a Daughter of Destiny? Are you a son of purpose? God wants you to know that He loves you. He has a good, perfect plan and purpose for your life. It may not be a straight line like you think it should be. It might have zigzag lines. It might have snags and loose threads running through it. It might have unforeseen threads of different shapes, colors, and sizes. But, when you turn the tapestry of your life around and see the other side, the side that God sees from His perspective, then you will see the beauty that He has made. God will reveal to you the masterpiece He is making of your life. He wants you to become a person of destiny and purpose.

Prayer:

Dear Lord,
Forgive me for thinking that what I've been through or am going through right now is only about me. Cause me to come up higher and see my circumstances from Your perspective. Thank You for working something beautiful out of my life. I believe that I have a purpose. I believe that I have a God-given destiny, and I choose to allow You to work out Your plan in my life. Amen.

Chapter Eight

Peace in the Storm

"Peace I leave with you, My peace I give to you;
not as the world gives do I give to you. Let not your
heart be troubled, neither let it be afraid"
John 14:27

Failed Marriage

Funny things about storms. A storm can be raging all around, with fierce winds and wild rains, but there is a place right in the middle of the storm where there is total calm and peace, with no wind and no rain. This is called the eye of the storm. It is in this eye that there is peace. In Matthew 14:22-32, the disciples were in a storm with high winds and big waves in the middle of the sea. Then, they saw Jesus walking toward them on the water, and they became frightened. But Jesus told

His disciples that it was He; they did not need to be afraid. Peter learned a valuable lesson that day. He learned that he could walk on water in the midst of a storm, but he was to keep his eyes on Jesus because he would sink the moment he took his eyes off of the Prince of Peace.

The lesson for us today is that there will be storms in our lives, but we are to keep looking at Jesus. He is the Prince of Peace, who brings and speaks peace to every storm. Wherever He is, no matter how fierce the storm, there is peace. On the day that the notice from the court came in the mail, a wild storm began in my heart, mind, and life. My husband was named as defendant in a paternity lawsuit, and he was ordered to pay child support. The child in question was already twelve years old—just six months older than my youngest son. It was not a mistake; the child was my husband's. The indiscretion had happened thirteen years prior, but I had just found out about it. The storm in my head was relentless. We talked and argued. I sought counsel, but he did not; I cried out to God in more pain.

The Bible says that, for the hardness of hearts, Moses allowed divorce, but in the beginning it was not so. Divorce was allowed only if there was adultery in the marriage. Clearly, I had grounds for divorce. However, I had previously learned to pray about everything. If you know anything about the God we serve, then you must know that nothing fazes Him; He never panics. I prayed and asked to be released from my marriage. Even though I had legal grounds—grounds even in the eyes of the church to divorce—what did God want from my life?

Nothing is as simple or clear cut as it might seem. God

said, "No. Do not depart, and do not divorce." He had other plans for me, and a divorce, at that time, was not part of them. I have often preached that forgiveness is not for the other person but for yourself. So, taking a page from one of my sermons, I asked the Lord to enable me to forgive. He did. He does still.

Application

Are you in a storm of life right now? Have you been dealt a devastating blow by a loved one? What's next? Do you curl up and die or commit suicide or a homicide? God forbid! Come to know the Peace Bringer—the One who calms every storm.

How do you have peace in a storm? First, recognize that storms come to anyone and everyone. No one is exempt from storms, especially not Christians. Sometimes, believers can hold the attitude that nothing bad should ever happen to them. And if something bad does happen, it's the person's own fault. You are the cause, or, worse yet, God must be punishing you for something you did. This attitude is not from the God we serve. Yes, there are consequences for bad choices and decisions, but God is not punishing you. The punishment for sin was dealt with over 2,000 years ago. Jesus took the punishment for our sins.

Sin is anything we do that displeases the Father. God showed His great love for us by having His son suffer and die for our punishment because we could not bear it ourselves. The miracle of Christianity is that Jesus overcame suffering, death, hell, and the grave; we become free and declared righteous by God when we accept Him as having taken our punishment. We are then declared in right standing with God. So, no, God is not punishing us when "bad" things happen. Rather, we are being refined—as gold is refined—in the fire. Our faith is tested and our character developed so that we begin to resemble the character of Christ. For when He was tested and tried, He did not sin. He did not become angry with God because He understood the purpose for the pain. He knew that God was not punishing Him but redeeming mankind through Him.

To have peace in the storm, believe that God is right there with you, and He will take you safely through every storm and adversity of life. As you thank Him for His presence and power in your life, you will have peace. Jesus said in John 14:27, "Peace I leave with you, My peace I give to you; not as the world gives do I give to you. Let not your heart be troubled, neither let it be afraid." Below is a poem I wrote during one of the many stormy seasons of my life:

The Storm is Almost Over
The storm is almost over.
Though the winds blow furiously
And the rain beat vehemently
Storm, you're almost over.

Satan, you may kick and scream,
But all that means
You know your time grows short.
Your storm is almost over.

I resist you in Jesus' Name.

This is your last-ditch game

For me to fear and flee,

But I won't agree – it's you who must flee.

I know the battle's not

With flesh and blood and all I see,

But a flood of spiritual wickedness

In Heavenly places is against me.

So the full armor of God I don

For the battle is to be won.

I'm covered in Jesus' Blood

So I can withstand the flood.

With heels dug in deep

It's God Word I will keep.

On His Word I stand alone

And having done all, I stand like stone.

I stand anyhow.

The storm's almost over.

I stand in spite of.

The storm's almost over.

God, my shield is He.

He guides, guards, and protects me.

He is my spiritual raincoat

And I'm well anchored in life's boat.

So when the rain beats down

The winds blow and all the more wail,

Right through I will sail.

The storm is almost over.

Prayer:

Dear Lord,

Thank You for being my peace in the midst of my storm. Whenever I am afraid, I will look to You and receive the peace that You give—peace that the world cannot take away. Carry me safely through this storm, and bring me to the other side in Jesus' Name. Amen.

Chapter Nine

A New Season

"Behold, I will do a new thing, Now it shall spring
forth; Shall you not know it?"
Isaiah 43:18

God's Release

I resisted divorce as a solution for many years because I knew that my marriage was ordained by God. The cuts served a purpose. Through the cuts in my marriage, I learned how to pray—really pray. I learned how to pray warfare prayers and how to intercede. I prayed for my husband diligently; I became an intercessor. As strange as it may sound, I often interceded for other couples and their marriages. My heart was broken over marriages that were on the brink of divorce or separation. I could feel the pain and hurt they were enduring, and it made me empathetic and compassionate toward them.

However, this was now a new season. It was time to go further, and I had to come to terms with my role as an enabler. I enabled my husband by seeking to keep the peace and not discussing the real issues of his deteriorating and self-sabotaging behavior with him. I had trusted God thus far, and now I had to trust Him the rest of the way. When God revealed to me it was time to separate from my husband, I resisted. I know that might seem strange to some, but I believe in marriage. I know that the enemy is the one who comes to steal, kill, and destroy. I had invested so many years in my marriage, praying for breakthrough and change, just to find out God wanted to change me. My change had come.

I asked God again for confirmation of this new season. He answered me by telling me to take my husband on a trip for his birthday. I was to celebrate with him by taking him to a place he wanted to go: Atlantic City. In the back of my mind, I was hopeful for my husband to change his pattern of self-destructive behavior, including overeating and not taking care of his body or health. However, when we arrived, I saw my husband continuing his indulgences while he knew fully that his behavior was killing him. Seeing this, it finally hit me that enough was enough. I was not his God or his savior. I had done all I possibly and humanly could do to help him, including scheduling many doctor's visits and staging interventions with his family and friends, who all told him the same thing: be willing to change your destructive behavior to save your health, mind, and marriage. He refused to listen to anyone, and now it was just between him and his God. I had to literally get out of the way to allow God to intervene in his life.

My decision to separate from my husband was made on the Atlantic City trip. When I got home, I knew what I had to do: get a lawyer, draft documents, and present them to my husband with a timetable for his departure. Was it easy? No, it was not. I cried throughout the whole experience. I was so distraught that I couldn't even pray with my prayer partners on my morning prayer line for a while. I just asked them to pray for me. Yet, once again, God made a way.

When the day came for my husband to leave, he left. It was just a month short of what would have been our thirtieth wedding anniversary. There was no scene as I had feared—no yelling or screaming. It was as if he knew that I'd had enough of living with him, and witnessing his slow death was no longer an option for me. It was not easy because the devil threw many accusations in my face:

What would your friends, family, and church say? How could you call yourself a pastor—a woman of God—and separate from your husband? Don't you have enough faith in God that He can rescue the marriage? Did God really bring you and your husband together? Did you make a mistake?

This was my internal monologue for many a day, until I remembered God's sovereignty. He had brought me this far. I had surrendered my life to Him a long time ago. Could I now go back and say, "Lord, I know I surrendered to you, but I only want the 'good parts' and none of the bad"? You know the answer to that one: "And we know that all things work together for good to those who love God, to those who are the called according to His purpose" (Romans 8:28). I had also learned that, even if I made a mistake, God would let me know in plenty of time to alter my course. I surrendered to God, once again, and welcomed a new season of my life.

Application

Has God asked you to do something that is emotionally hard to do? Have you hesitated to do it? Has He asked you to have a difficult conversation with a family member or friend? Has He asked you to stop being an enabler? Did He take off your mask and expose you to yourself? As I have said before, God will never lead you to something that He will not bring you through. The mountain may be high and the climb long and steep, but God is right there with you every step of the way. He will give you hinds' feet to leap, skip, and jump over every mountain (Habakkuk 3:19). Make up your mind to trust God with every ounce of your being.

People might talk negatively about you for following God or for the godly decision you made, but remember that they have no heaven or hell to put you in. You must answer to God yourself for all you have done in the body and for every idle word that proceeds out of your mouth (Matthew 12:36). Do not allow family or friends to influence you when you know—through prayer, Bible reading, and godly advice—that this is what God would have you to do. The decisions that you've made should result in your peace of mind, not in anxiety, worry, or fear.

Prayer:

Dear Lord,

I believe that I am walking into a new season in my life—a season of fulfillment and peace. Help me to make the right decisions and hard choices. May my life be honoring to You in my words, thoughts, and deeds. Amen.

Chapter Ten

———◆◆◆———

God Heals the Brokenhearted

"Is there no balm in Gilead? Is there no physician there? Why then has not the [spiritual] health of the daughter of my people been restored?"
Jeremiah 8:21-22 (Amplified Bible)

Apply the BALM

Brokenhearted Heart

Lord, You who heal the brokenhearted
Heal my broken heart.
I know I'm called in Your Name
Liberty for the captives to proclaim.

But Lord, first I must be free.
For how can I heal the broken hearted
With a brokenhearted heart?

Lord, how can I set captives free
From prison walls and cells
When the same walls
Surround, bind, and imprison me?

Oh Lord, how I long for Your breakthrough
Your change that really is change.
How I long for prison walls
To crumble and fall
Once and for all.

Lord, I am willing
Set me free, I pray.
I repent for every pity party
For every hasty word spoken
Contrary to Your Word.

I want to touch the brokenhearted.
Lord, heal my brokenhearted heart.
I want to bring prisoners to victory.
Lord, release me from every captivity.

I know it's not by might
I know it's not by power

I know Your Spirit rules the day.
Lord, guide, guard, and protect me in Your way.

I will be free.
I will prison doors release.
Captives of all kinds
Get ready to walk in freedom and peace.

I will be bold.
I will be made whole.
I will heal the brokenhearted
With a healed brokenhearted heart

Years ago, during turbulent times in my marriage, as I cried out to God, He told me that He would use me to heal the brokenhearted. My response to Him was defiant: "How can I heal the brokenhearted with a brokenhearted heart?"

I wrote the above poem around that time. I was still learning that God's view of things was different from mine. God did not waver in what He told me; He did not change His mind. It was up to me to give in and surrender to my destiny. Yes, I was brokenhearted, but God heals the brokenhearted. I have experienced both the breaking and the remaking of my heart. In doing so, God has given me compassion for the broken, the down and out, and those who feel that all hope is gone.

I am passionate about letting people know that God heals the brokenhearted. Jeremiah was a prophet of God, and

God gave him a burden for people. He said:

> For the brokenness of the daughter of my people I
> (Jeremiah) am broken;
> I mourn, anxiety has gripped me.
> Is there no balm in Gilead?
> Is there no physician there?
> Why then has not the [spiritual] health of the daughter of
> my people been restored?
> (Jeremiah 8:21-22, Amplified Bible)

Jeremiah asked if there was no balm in Gilead, no medicine, and no cure for the recovery of the brokenness of the daughters of Zion. He said that he was broken over their brokenness. To answer Jeremiah's question: Yes, there is a balm in Gilead. There is recovery for the daughters of Zion and the Daughters of Destiny. I say to you today, no matter what trial, tribulation, hardship, challenge, or difficulty you have faced or are facing right now in life, Jesus is your balm in Gilead.

What is a balm? The balm of Gilead was a fragrant ointment or preparation used to heal or soothe the skin. It was a rare perfume used medicinally and named for the region of Gilead, where it was produced. It has come to signify a universal cure. So, when Jeremiah says there is a balm in Gilead, God is saying there is healing for His people and, in particular, for His precious daughters.

I believe that God has given women great empathy and compassion for others naturally; unfortunately, that also puts us in a position of being hurt or deceived. We tend to think the best of others. We tend to think that others would do for us what we would do for them. However, if you've lived long enough, you know this is not true. Women mostly tend to be trusting, and that puts us in the position of having our hearts broken. We suffer rejection and disappointment. We have also faced abuse in our lives, whether physical, sexual, emotional, mental, spiritual, or even financial. We might think, *Well, God does not love me* because the enemy puts that in our minds. We may say, "If God loved me, why would He have allowed this to happen?" The enemy said to me: "If God loved you, your marriage would not have failed." We might even buy into the enemy's lies for a time and get mad at God for what we think isn't fair in life. But God does love us, and what has happened in our lives—no matter how horrific or sorrowful—still has a purpose. God loves you. He shares in your infirmities. What hurts you, hurts Jesus.

When God released me from my marriage and allowed me to separate from my husband, the marriage was just a month short of lasting thirty years. It was a toxic and abusive relationship for most of those years. However, over the years, God consistently applied the balm to my heart. He kept showing me His love, despite my feeling unloved by my own husband. God reminded me of a scripture He had given me before I was married or had even met my husband. Isaiah 54:5 says that the Lord God is our husband. God told me then that He would be better to me than a husband—even better to me than my children.

God healed me from the wounds inflicted in my

marriage. The healing was not all at once, but it was gradual. The last bit of healing came after my release from the marriage. I know that I am healed because I am able to write this book. Before, I never wanted to talk about or even share what was happening in my marriage out of embarrassment. Further, you know the old devil line, "What will people say," not to mention the fact that sharing made me depressed. I couldn't even talk about it without crying. I only shared a small part of what was happening in my marriage with prayer partners and godly pastors so that they could pray. I never shared my situation with family, church members, or casual friends.

I carried around a lot of emotional baggage. My self-esteem was low, and I felt emotionally drained. Have you ever felt like you were not good enough, not smart enough, or not capable enough? I had defeating and debilitating thoughts of self-blame. I looked back at a failed marriage and wondered: What went wrong? How was I to blame? I thought, *If only I did this or that*, but I knew, when I'd done all I humanly could and was unable to fix the problem, I had to then allow the Master Fixer to step in and take over.

God wants to free His Daughters of Destiny from all debilitating thoughts and negative patterns that come to steal, kill, and destroy—thoughts that steal your happiness, kill your confidence, and destroy your peace. He wants you to focus on and cultivate your God-given talents, gifts, and abilities and work toward emotional wholeness.

I had to learn not to allow my emotions to dictate decisions in the heat of a moment. I learned how to guard my tongue and think before I spoke. I learned how to stop rehearsing scenarios in my head and worrying about how a difficult conversation would go before it even happened. I dreaded the conversation I would have to have with my husband about separating and the timeframe I gave him to leave. And yet, when the conversation finally came, it was not the horror that I had envisioned. My husband agreed that we should separate, and he left. None of the fuss, drama, or scenes that I spent time worrying about happened. God had mercy on us both, and I knew this was the right thing to do.

My healing was completed after I separated from my husband. It gave me time to breathe without walking on eggshells—too afraid to speak or be myself. It allowed me precious quiet time to hear my own thoughts. It was only after the separation that I became a published author. I had begun writing the book *The Well Woman* many years prior to its release in 2020, but I never had the time, confidence, or, to be quite honest, the motivation to complete it. I kept thinking to myself, *How in the world am I a well woman?* Yet, when the time came to finish and publish it, I had indeed become a well woman. God had healed my broken heart, and I was asked to heal the brokenhearted.

If you feel brokenhearted, cry out to God for healing; He heals the brokenhearted. A broken and contrite heart He will not despise (Psalm 51:17). I challenge you today to have a real conversation with the living God. Then, I ask you to do something simple but powerful: apply the BALM of Gilead to your life. BALM stands for Blessed Almighty Loves Me.

In other words, you, yes you, are blessed, meaning that you are happy, fortunate, and are to be envied. Why? Because the Lord God Almighty loves you (John 3:16). Accept that God loves you even with all your flaws, insecurities, and hang-ups. Come to Him just as you are and allow His BALM to bring you healing in your mind, body, soul, and spirit.

Application

Apply the BALM to your life. Get a new bottle of olive oil. The oil represents the Holy Spirit present in your life to heal, deliver, and set you free. Pray over the oil in the name of Jesus, then follow the instructions for anointing yourself. Believe God as you use the consecrated oil to set yourself free in your mind, emotions, spirit, body, and even your finances. Believe God that there is recovery for the brokenness of His people. The first recovery is your relationship with God. If you have never asked Jesus to come into your heart to be your Lord and Savior, do this first before you apply the BALM. Now is the day of salvation. Repeat the following simple prayer if you want to receive Jesus:

Prayer:

Lord Jesus,
I repent of anything I might have done to displease You in thought, word, or deed. I believe that You died on the cross, so that I might live. Jesus, come into my life. I commit my life

to you, confessing You as my Lord and Savior. I receive Your forgiveness. I receive Your healing. Teach me how to live for You each new day. Amen.

Apply the Physical BALM

Anoint yourself by dabbing a little bit of the consecrated oil on the following parts of your body as a point of contact for your faith and to represent God's deliverance in each of these areas:

Eyes
- Revelation 3:18: "... anoint your eyes with eye salve, that you may see ..."
- Ask God for spiritual discernment to see clearly what He is doing in your life.
- Repent from any backsliding or from being a carnal Christian.

Say: *"In the Name of Jesus, I decree and declare that I see clearly the Gospel of Jesus Christ."*

Top of Head
- 2 Corinthians 5:17: "Therefore, if anyone is in Christ, he is a new creation; old things have passed away; behold, all things have become new."
- Know that you are saved. Put on the helmet of salvation.

Say: *"In the Name of Jesus, I decree and declare that I am saved. I am a new creation in Christ Jesus. The old has passed, and the new is here."*

Forehead

- 1 Corinthians 2:16: "But we have the mind of Christ."
- Ask God to heal your mind of wounds from the past and present.
- Ask Him to enable you to think rationally and clearly.
- Confess that you are free from past hurts and pains and that you will no longer rehearse the pain over and over in your mind.
- Believe that you will sleep well at night without tossing
  and turning because of worry.
- Replace every negative and derogatory thought of yourself, your situation, or your circumstance with the thoughts of God and with the Word of God.
- Set your thoughts on things that are just, pure, peaceable, and praiseworthy (Philippians 4:8).
- Give it all to Jesus. You may never get an apology from your abuser, but let it go.

Say: *"In the Name of Jesus, I decree and declare that I have the mind of Christ; I speak healing to my mind."*

Mouth/Tongue

- James 3:10-12: "Out of the same mouth proceed blessing and cursing. My brethren, these things ought not to be so. Does a spring send forth fresh water and bitter from the same opening? Can a fig tree, my brethren, bear olives, or a grapevine bear figs? Thus no spring yields both salt water and fresh."

- Ask God to deliver you from doublespeak.
- Do not allow any unwholesome words to come out of your mouth.
- Ask that the words of your mouth be acceptable to God (Psalm 19:14).

Say: *"Lord, as I anoint my mouth, I declare deliverance from doublespeak. I speak life only and not death."*

Chest (Heart)

- Isaiah 61:1:

  The Spirit of the Lord God is upon Me,

  Because the Lord has anointed Me

  To preach good tidings to the poor;

  He has sent Me to heal the brokenhearted,

  To proclaim liberty to the captives,

  And the opening of the prison

  to those who are bound.

- Ask God for emotional healing.
- Ask God to heal your broken heart.

Say: *"I am set free this day, healed in every place where I am emotionally broken."*

Stomach

- Isaiah 53:5: "But He was wounded for our transgressions, He was bruised for our iniquities; The chastisement for our peace *was* upon Him, and by His stripes we are healed."
- 1 Peter 2:24 ". . . who Himself bore our sins in His own body on the tree, that we, having died to sins, might live for righteousness—by whose stripes you were healed."
- Ask God for physical healing.
- Ask God for healing from physical abuse.

Say: *"I appropriate the finished work of Calvary to my body this day. By Jesus' stripes, I am healed."*

Hips

- John 8:10-12:

  When Jesus had raised Himself up and saw no one but the woman, He said to her, 'Woman, where are those accusers of yours? Has no one condemned you?' She said, 'No one, Lord.' And Jesus said to her, 'Neither do I condemn you; go and sin no more.' Then Jesus spoke to them again, saying, 'I am the light of the world. He who follows Me shall not walk in darkness but have the light of life.'

- Romans 8:1-2:

  There is therefore now no condemnation to those who are in Christ Jesus, who do not walk according to the flesh, but according to the Spirit. For the law of the Spirit of life in Christ Jesus has made me free from the law of sin and death.

- Ask God for sexual healing if you have been raped, sexually abused, or assaulted.
- Recognize that it's not your fault. Let go of the guilt and shame.

Say: *"I walk in the light. Light exposes the dark. I am free from all of the hidden, dark places in my life. I am not condemned."*

Legs

- Ephesians 6:10-15:

    Finally, my brethren, be strong in the Lord and in the power of His might. Put on the whole armor of God, that you may be able to stand against the wiles of the devil. For we do not wrestle against flesh and blood, but against principalities, against powers, against the rulers of the darkness of this age, against spiritual hosts of wickedness in the heavenly places. Therefore take up the whole armor of God, that you may be able to withstand in the evil day, and having done all, to stand.

- Stand up for Jesus; be a witness.
- Believe that God will give you what to say and how to say it.

Say: *"I stand up for righteousness. I stand against all the assignments of the enemy to steal, kill, and destroy my life. I stand strong in the Lord and in the power of His might."*

Hands

- Deuteronomy 8:18: "And you shall remember the LORD your God, for it is He who gives you power to get ‹ wealth."
- Deuteronomy 30:9:

    The LORD your God will make you abound in all the work of your hand, in the fruit of your body, in the increase of your livestock, and in the produce of your land for good.

- Ask God for financial healing and wisdom in dealing with your finances.
- Give to godly ministries.
- Give to the needy.
- Obey what God tells you to do.

Say: *"I have, in my hands, the power to create wealth. I give to others freely and cheerfully in Jesus' Name. I prosper in whatever I put my hands to do."*

Feet

- Ephesians 6:15: "... and having shod your feet with the preparation of the gospel of peace."
- Isaiah 52:7:

    How beautiful upon the mountains are the feet of him who brings good news, who proclaims peace, who brings glad tidings of good things, who proclaims salvation, who says to Zion, 'Your God reigns!'

Say: *"My feet are always at the right place at the right time. I will use my feet to go tell what God has done for me. I will share my testimony."*

Apply the Spiritual BALM

As you have applied the BALM in the natural (to your physical self), so now you must also apply the BALM in the supernatural by speaking out loud to the issues in the following areas. Speak the BALM over whichever applies to your life and/or situation.

As you apply the balm to the following areas, repeat out loud: *"I apply the BALM in the Name of Jesus. I am healed, and I am free."*

Every Type of Abuse

- Physical, sexual, emotional, mental, and financial.
- If you were the abuser: of yourself, your children, your parents, or your spouse.

Say: *"I apply the BALM in the Name of Jesus. I am healed, and I am free."*

Relationship Issues

- Toxic relationships between: spouse, parent or child, boss or employee, minister or congregant.
- Ungodly emotional connections.
- Stalking or intimidation.
- Manipulation or controlling behavior.
- Emotional chains.

Say: *"I apply the BALM in the Name of Jesus. I am healed, and I am free."*

Mental Health Issues

- Depression, discouragement, and suicidal thoughts.
- Unreasonable fears, phobias, self-doubt, and low self-esteem.
- Soul ties, strongholds, and mental bondages.
- Confusion of the mind.

Say: *"I apply the BALM in the Name of Jesus. I am healed, and I am free."*

Emotional Issues

- Anger, rage, bad temper, irritability, meanness, resentment, and bitterness.
- Unforgiveness, envy, jealousy, malice, and greed.
- Lust, shame, guilt, and condemnation.
- Self-centeredness, loneliness, and emotional triggers.

Say: *"I apply the BALM in the Name of Jesus. I am healed, and I am free."*

Issues of the Tongue and Self-Control

- Slander, lying, obscenity, abusive, filthy, vulgar language, and profanity.
- Negative self-talk.

Say: *"I apply the BALM in the Name of Jesus. I am healed, and I am free."*

All Forms and Expressions of Self-Hatred and Addictions

- Self-harm and mutilation.

- Addictions: drugs, smoking, pornography, social media, shopping, and food.

Say: *"I apply the BALM in the Name of Jesus. I am healed, and I am free."*

Sexual Perversions

- Immorality, impurity, sinful passions, evil desires, and gender confusion.
- Infidelity.

Say: *"I apply the BALM in the Name of Jesus. I am healed, and I am free."*

Family & Generational issues

- Family secrets, incest, betrayal, foster care, adoption, divorce, separations, and adultery.
- Generational curses and transfer of spirits.

Say: *"I apply the BALM in the Name of Jesus. I am healed, and I am free."*

All Types of Peer Issues

- Bullying, non-acceptance, teasing, and taunting.

Say: *"I apply the BALM in the Name of Jesus. I am healed, and I am free."*

All Types of Learning Disabilities

- Attention deficit disorder and hyperactivity.
- Dyslexia and autism.

Say: *"I apply the BALM in the Name of Jesus. I am healed, and I am free."*

Physical Bodily Issues

• All sickness, illness, and diseases.

Say: *"I apply the BALM in the Name of Jesus. I am healed, and I am free."*

Spiritual Issues

• Nonexistent or wrong relationship with God; no intimacy with God.
• Wrong concepts of God or thinking God is mad at you.
• Religion over relationship with God.
• Religious mentality or spirit.
• Disobedience to God.
• Church hurt.

Say: *"I apply the BALM in the Name of Jesus. I am healed, and I am free."*

Praise God for the victory in your life. Praise Him for healing the brokenhearted and apply the BALM every day:

Blessed

Almighty

Loves

Me

Chapter Eleven

The Power of Forgiveness

"Then Jesus said, 'Father, forgive them, for they do not know what they do.'"
Luke 23:34

Made Whole in Mind, Body, Soul, and Spirit

I've been well-trained in forgiveness. It's not that I've forgiven my husband only now. No, every time there was an offense, God asked me to forgive him. My act of forgiveness wasn't so much about my husband's relief as much as it was for my healing. To say forgiveness came easy is an understatement. Forgiveness was far from easy, but in living a surrendered life to God, it didn't matter if it was hard to do; it was a necessity. If I claim to be a follower of Christ, then forgiving others of their offenses against me is necessary.

Did Jesus not lead the way in forgiveness? Did He not

teach us and give us direct instructions on forgiveness? Yes, He did, but it doesn't make it easy. Forgiveness can be unpleasant, especially when you believe you're the one who has been wronged. Jesus once asked His disciples how many times they thought that they should forgive. It was really a pop quiz. Would they get it right after spending all that time with Him? The disciples had been under his teaching for almost three years, and He taught them to forgive. He was going to make the ultimate sacrifice, and He had to know that they would forgive His abusers.

Peter thought he was being generous when he offered to forgive seven times (Matthew 18:21-22). When Jesus said no, not seven times, but seventy-times-seven, He didn't mean to literally forgive four hundred-and-ninety times. Rather, Jesus was saying to forgive as often as there is an offense. He also said that, if we don't forgive, neither will our Heavenly Father forgive us. In fact, since God has forgiven us our trespasses, who are we not to forgive those who trespass against us? Jesus taught His disciples this when He demonstrated how to pray effectively.

From the cross, Jesus spoke to the Father, asking for forgiveness for those who were crucifying Him. He forgave those who nailed Him to the cross, those who taunted Him, and those who set Him up for punishment with false accusations: "Father, forgive them." He told the Father that "they know not what they do" (Luke 23:34). They didn't know that they were crucifying their own long-awaited Messiah. Obviously this was all part of God's perfect, divine plan.

No matter how bleak the situation looks, no matter how broken you might feel, God always has a plan. He is the Potter, and we are the clay. Jesus' forgiveness was not just for those who plotted against Him, and it was not only for those who nailed Him to a tree. Forgiveness was extended that day to all those who brought Him to that cross because of their sins: you and I. In the garden before His arrest, Jesus prayed: "Father, if it is Your will take this cup away from Me" (Luke 22:42). What Jesus had to do, including enduring cruel beatings and scourging, was hard. The flesh revolted at the very prospect of it, but Jesus left us a clear example when He said: "nevertheless not My will, but Yours be done" (Luke 22:42). Forgiveness is powerful.

Staying in constant communication with the Lord enabled me to forgive not just once; but the full seventy-times-seven concept. If I stubbornly refused to forgive, I'd get a tinge in my stomach—a knowing in my knower—to recognize that I was wrong to do so. Jesus said, "For if you forgive men their trespasses, your heavenly Father will also forgive you. But if you do not forgive men their trespasses, neither will your Father forgive your trespasses" (Matthew 6:14-15). I could not minister with unforgiveness in my heart. My slate had to be clean to be able to lay hands on people and speak into their lives, saying, "Thus says the Spirit of the Living God." If I wasn't going to listen to the Spirit of the Living God for myself, how could I possible hear what He was saying to others?

My prayer life would also have been hindered if I did not forgive. I learned that God will not speak beyond the last thing He told you to do if you do not do that thing. No next steps will be given if you didn't take the first steps. I constantly walked in a state of forgiveness. As I said, it was not easy. One day in particular, an unexpected offense occurred as soon as I walked into the door of my apartment. I quickly retreated to my bedroom to be alone. I didn't even take off my coat, but I knelt down next to my bed and literally stayed on my knees for about twenty minutes, allowing God to work forgiveness out within me before I could dare to open my mouth and speak to my husband.

I often wrestled with unforgiveness, but trying to justify my unforgiveness to a forgiving God was futile. So, in times when forgiving was especially tough, I prayed and asked the Holy Spirit to forgive through me. Each time, He enabled me to let it go and forgive. Holding unforgiveness in your heart really does damage to yourself, not the other person. You know the famous saying: Not forgiving is like you taking poison and expecting the other person to die. If you are holding on to unforgiveness, you're killing yourself. In our society today, some family members have stopped speaking to one another, refusing to forgive some offenses. They hold on to grudges and long-standing feuds. When the newer generation asks what the feud is about, no one can say because it was some distant offense of which no one can remember the details. All they know is that they're not speaking to "Uncle John" or "Aunt Jane."

Forgiveness is so powerful that it can make you whole. If you want to be made whole in your mind, body, soul, and spirit, forgive. I can't stress it enough. There is much power in forgiving an offense and releasing the offender. When you forgive, you stop the offender from hurting you again and again long after the offense is over. Conversely, holding on to unforgiveness can make you sick spiritually, mentally, emotionally, and even physically.

Application

If you have been offended (let's be real, we all have), then search your heart. If you are holding unforgiveness toward anyone, stop right now. Acknowledge it. Acknowledge it as sin, then ask the Holy Spirit to forgive through you. Yield to the Spirit of Christ and be willing to say "yes" to the process. As you forgive, you will break chains off your mind, and you will unshackle your ability to hear clearly from God and be used by Him.

The offending party may never apologize or even acknowledge that they have offended you, but forgive them anyway. How do you know you've really forgiven someone of an offense? You can be certain of your forgiveness when you can look at that offense or person and no longer harbor feelings of rage, anger, bitterness, or resentment. You have really forgiven when you don't get sick to your stomach at the thought of the offense. Freely you have received forgiveness, so freely give it as well. Ephesians tells us, "Let all bitterness, wrath, anger, clamor, and evil speaking be put away from you, with all malice. And be kind to one another tenderhearted, forgiving one

another, even as God in Christ forgave you" (Ephesians 4:31-
32).

Prayer:

Dear Lord,

*Thank You for forgiving me of all my offenses against You. I
ask You to forgive through me. Allow me to forgive others their
offenses against me and cause me to walk daily in an attitude of
forgiveness. I recognize that there is great power in forgiveness.
I forgive now all who have offended me, thereby releasing
myself from any bondage of unforgiveness. Teach me how to be
kind and loving toward others. Amen.*

Chapter Twelve

The Wounded Healer

"The Spirit of the Lord God is upon Me,
Because the Lord has anointed Me
To preach good tidings to the poor;
He has sent Me to heal the brokenhearted,
To proclaim liberty to the captives,
And the opening of the prison to those who are
bound."
Isaiah 61:1

Where I Am Today

There is certainly a BALM in Gilead. I am living proof of this. God has restored the years the locust and cankerworm hath eaten. He has hastened to perform His good Word over me. Over the years, I've given God the little that I've had, and

He's made it grand. He has called me to preach the Good News, and He has used me to heal the brokenhearted and proclaim liberty to the captives. I am grateful for all that the Lord has allowed me to go through because it has made me the woman I am today. The pain I suffered allowed me to give birth to the Daughters of Destiny Ministry and minister with empathy and compassion to the lost, lonely, rejected, and discouraged.

Today, I have a women's empowerment ministry, and I minister in my local church. I am a mother to two adult sons and two daughters-in-love. I am a retired public school teacher, a pastor, an author, a women's conference host and speaker, and an encourager to many. I thank God for my ministry, Daughters of Destiny, and the work He has allowed me to do in my local church.

I'm including in this chapter a few testimonies from those whose lives have been impacted by my ministry, both men and women, as God is not a respecter of persons. I include them as a testimony to what God can do with little when it is in His Hands. I accept no glory for myself, but I give it all to God. I share these testimonies as encouragement to you, wherever you are in life. If you are in a difficult relationship or circumstance, do not give up or lose faith. Allow God to work out His perfect plan in your life. Remember that God still heals, still delivers, and still sets free. I thank God for the Kingdom work He has allowed me to do and for the books He has enabled me to write thus far. I look forward to doing more for the Most High.

I want to thank all those who gave testimonies. Whether

you know it or not, you are a part of my journey and further proof that God is with me. You are proof that God took the little that I had and made it grand. God has promised to never leave me nor forsake me. I look forward to the more that He has in store. Shalom.

Testimonies to the Glory of God

"Praise the Lord! My name is Karen Brown, and I'm privileged to have been a participant of the Daughters of Destiny yearly conferences! From its very inception, Pastor Barfield included me and the Sisters in the Gap prayer group to intercede for the conference and its participants that God's anointing be all over and in it! God always showed up and showed out! This conference has impacted my life in so many ways—in [the] areas of finance, marriage, gifts and callings, and especially prayer! Nobody leaves that conference the same as they came! And that's the focus! CHANGE! I thank God for allowing Pastor to flourish in this ministry, and I pray that it continues until the Lord comes!"

Karen Brown, Georgia

"Pastor Barfield has been a tremendous joy in my life. Her ministry has blessed me in ways I can't even begin to explain. I remember prophetic words she's spoken over my life that have come to pass. I thank God immensely for her walking in her purpose. Beyond her ministry, Pastor Barfield has been a shoulder to lean on and a sound voice of wisdom. If you ever have the opportunity to be in her presence, please take the time to learn and grow from her. Thank you, Pastor Barfield, for being such a blessing to my life!"

Nikkie Pryce, Florida

"Pastor Heather Barfield has been an angel in my life for 42 years. We first met at age 8 when my mom married her brother. She was the person to give me my first Bible and was a very special aunt, who taught me about the deep love that GOD has for us and how following the teachings of Jesus Christ would help me live a deeply fulfilled life. For many years, we lost touch, but recently we reconnected. And she has added a spark of joy to my life with her wisdom and prayer. I read her book Meeting God Daily every morning as part of my morning routine, and I feel blessed to have the opportunity to know her, pray with her, and learn from her. She is wisdom in motion, and we all are fortunate to have her as a resource."

Isaac Molina, California

"I have known Pastor Heather Barfield for nearly 40 years, and throughout those years, she has been a constant blessing to me, my family, and to the Body of Christ. Yes, God has blessed her with many ministry gifts, but I've been a witness to her transparent and caring heart. Through Pastor Barfield's obedience in creating and maintaining Daughters of Destiny Ministry, she presents a platform that empowers women with opportunities to develop and share their ministry gifts. I believe Daughters of Destiny is doing just as God intends it to do: 'enable, equip and encourage women to enter into their divinely appointed destinies.' Many of these women have blossomed and gone on to be a blessing to others. By the grace of God, I am one such woman. To God be the Glory!"

Chaplain Carolyn Davis, New York

"I am not a daughter of destiny, but I'm a man of destiny. My wife is a daughter of destiny. Our 15-year-old granddaughter is a daughter of destiny. My two sisters are daughters of destiny. I have been fortunate enough to attend Daughter of Destiny events, and the uplifting and healing experience has truly blessed me."

Aubrey D. Evelyn, Esq., Maryland

"Pastor Heather Barfield and Daughters of Destiny Ministry have impacted and blessed many women through the years. I am grateful that Pastor Barfield has been a blessing to me as a mentor, ministry partner, and has ministered at the annual Women of Influence Empowerment Network (WIEN) Retreat for over ten years. Through her ministry, I have seen women healed, encouraged, and challenged to a deeper relationship with Christ. Pastor Barfield is a teacher who emphasizes biblical integrity. She has been an integral part of my continued growth and maturity in ministry. Paul writes in Ephesians 2:10 that we are God's workmanship, created to do good works. Only eternity will tell the true impact of Pastor Barfield's work through Daughters of Destiny."

Pastor Marcia Walker, Ohio

"Pastor Heather Barfield demonstrates the heart of Jesus in who she is and in how she ministers. As we've served together over the years, I find her life's passion is a real desire to reach the people around her with the overwhelming, healing love of Jesus Christ. In regard to Daughters of Destiny, I can only tell

of what I experienced . . . The power of God alive and present in the word that was preached, a word that both challenged and freed me! This ministry is all about cultivating the greatness in the women who attend and empowering them to overcome the obstacles engineered to overcome them. Heather is simply interested in seeing people, women in particular, live their most abundant lives, body-soul-spirit. As her friend and fellow minister for Daughters of Destiny, I'm more poised for my purpose due to my participation in it. This dynamic ministry, birthed from her great vision, is equipping women with the courage to lay hold of the design for which God created them."

Cherette White, New York

"I attended the Daughters of Destiny Conference without a thought of what to expect, but I knew one thing: my pastor [and mentor], Heather Barfield, is a phenomenal woman of God, so something amazing was going to happen. My takeaway from the conference and what became a chain breaker for me was about my identity and who I am identified with. This helped me to realize what is important to me as a Christian and how I live my life. As a Christian, my identity must come from my relationship with my Abba Father, and this is what Daughters of Destiny did for me. I recognized my true identity being a daughter of the Most High, a Daughter of Destiny. I left the conference spiritually filled, renewed, rejuvenated, and wanting more."

Sunita Jaundoo-Frank, New York

"Reverend Barfield's ministry has been a blessing to me and my family. Her message has always been one of encouragement and empowerment. She encourages us to build our faith by regularly reading God's Word. Armed with God's Word, we are strengthened and able to meet daily challenges. Her Daughters of Destiny Ministry teaches that we are blessed by God's grace, and as such, the power we need to live happy, healthy, productive lives is already in us if we are open to accept it."

Marcia Murrell, New York

"Daughters of Destiny is a safe space for women to pour out their hearts. It's a place where their voices can be heard, and [it is] a place where they are allowed to feel without shame and guilt. Over the years, I attended countless Christian conferences, conventions, retreats, all night prayer meetings, shut-ins, etc. I have grown, matured and been blessed. However, I can still remember the first Daughters of Destiny Conference I attended. It was an encounter with God. To this day, it remains a life-changing experience. I was certain that I would return the next year and the year after that. Daughters of Destiny is the annual conference I look forward to because I know there will be sisterly love awaiting. Pastor Heather Barfield, the founder of Daughters of Destiny, has truly captured God's vision and purpose for women!"

Judith Daniels, New York

"What can I say about Daughters of Destiny? This ministry is spearheaded by Heather Barfield, a true woman of God. Her persistent faith in the Lord and her confidence of what God can do is contagious. There is no way that you can be connected to Pastor Barfield or this ministry and not be elevated. Daughters of Destiny has been such a blessing in various ways. One of the ways Daughters of Destiny has impacted me is by being a safe space to just BE. I was encouraged to be my authentic self, as well as operate in the gifts God has given me. The support from this ministry has boosted my confidence and, in many ways, strengthened my relationship with the Lord. I am so glad that I am forever connected with Pastor Barfield and Daughters of Destiny!"

Candice Hudson, New York

"I rejoice in the Lord because of the Daughters of Destiny Conferences. God has blessed me to attend for six years, invite others, and to listen to the anointed word and music. The presence of the Lord is there, and you can feel it in the atmosphere. Praise God."

Beverly Davie, New York

"I am thankful for the ministry of Pastor Heather Barfield and Daughters of Destiny. She is a mighty woman of God who is passionate about winning souls for Christ and seeing others walk in their God-given purpose. I have experienced that firsthand with the prayers she has offered up for me and the breakthroughs I have experienced. I was also delighted

to be a speaker alongside her at her Daughters of Destiny women's conference. It was [a] time of refreshing and miracles in sharing and receiving from the Lord. Her books are very inspiring. I was blessed to do the endorsement on the back cover of her book, <u>The Well Woman</u>. I am even more blessed to have her as one of the co-authors in the book that I compiled, <u>Resilient Faith: Dare to Believe</u>. Her stories and ministry are life-transforming."

Min. Rhonda P. Fraser, New York

"From the conception, I knew Daughters of Destiny was special. My first memory of the service felt like I was just beginning to conceive my own walk with God. I was at an early age in life during the first service; aware enough to perceive the events around me, and yet still naïve enough to not fully grasp the gravity of it all. I watched women commune with God in a way I'd never seen before. From the birth of Daughters of Destiny, there was an anointing over the room that was felt by all. From the first service, I watched the seed planted in that room grow into more services, more events, and more anointings. As I grew alongside, no longer naïve to the situation, I knew being a part of this ministry was the least I could do. I loved being a part of renewing people's lives when they came to this event. You see, when you watch a seed grow, it compels you to plant more seeds, and that was exactly what Daughters of Destiny was doing, planting seeds into people's lives everywhere."

Nilee Barfield, New York

"Daughters of Destiny Ministry is a godly women's empowerment ministry, which has transformed the lives of many over the years. I've witnessed hundreds of women grow spiritually, emotionally, and even mentally. Using the tools and knowledge they learned from Pastor Barfield's signature Daughters of Destiny Conference and the many books she has written, countless testimonies have come forward of women who've been inspired to start their own ministries. The Daughters of Destiny Conference is and will forever be my go-to conference every year. As I grow spiritually, I continue to incorporate the devotional: 'Meeting God Daily: Encouragement for Each New Day' in my 21-day fast every January. Pastor Heather Barfield has been an inspiration to me and to others, and I can't wait to see what God has in store for her in the future."

Justin Barfield, New York

Closing Thoughts

As believers, we should never assume that, once we are born again, our lives should have a smooth and straight path. God often tells us to do hard things that He, of course, already knows the outcome of. In life, you will find that it is not only about the destination but also the journey. We must be careful not to box God into our idea of who He is. We can't restrict His plans for what our lives should look like. After all, Joseph was chosen and loved by God. God revealed to him that he would be great, yet the path to getting there didn't seem to make any sense. He was sold into slavery by his own brothers, wrongfully accused by his boss, and put into a prison, seemingly left to rot away into obscurity. God's idea of how His plan should be executed is different than ours. Joseph learned that, where others meant to do him evil, God meant it for good. It was all for a purpose. God had a plan.

I want to encourage you that, no matter what you may have gone through or are going through right now, God still has a plan. His plans are only good. I encourage you not to curse God and die but to trust Him with all of your heart. Lean not unto your own understanding, but acknowledge Him in all your ways, and He will direct your paths (Proverbs 3:5-6). I encourage you to surrender your life fully to God. Give Him the little that you have and see how He will make it grand.

If you are not a believer, then what are you waiting for? Today is the day of salvation. Go back, reread the prayer in chapter one, and ask God to reveal Himself to you. He will. Enjoy the journey.

About the Author

Pastor Heather Barfield has been ministering the Word of God for over twenty-five years. She has taught God's Word to all ages and has seen lives transformed through the reading and study of the Word of God.

Pastor Barfield speaks, ministers, preaches, and teaches at various events, including women's conferences, prayer retreats, church functions, and women's meetings. She hosts annual women's conferences through her ministry, Daughters of Destiny, in which she enables, equips, and encourages women to enter into their divinely-appointed destinies.

She operates in a strong prophetic anointing, and God uses her to speak life into the lives of women who have been battered or abused physically, mentally, emotionally, and even spiritually.

Pastor Barfield is the author of two other books: *Meeting God Daily*, a 52-week devotional designed to bring the reader into a closer walk with God; and *The Well Woman*, a book that takes the reader on a life-changing journey of healing and restoration.

Pastor Barfield is also a contributing author of three other books:

Resilient Faith: Dare to Believe, a collection of testimonials of faith by women leaders.

Let the Women Speak: Unleashing Women to Turn Their Wounds into Wisdom, powerful stories of women sharing about life's struggles and successes.

Taking Care of Our Mental Health – From a Christian Perspective, an intimate and transparent exchange for believers wresting with mental health issues.

For more information about her ministry, events, and conferences, please visit: heatherbarfieldministries.com.

ARE YOU A WOUNDED HEALER IN NEED OF PRAYER?

Do you seek clarity for the situations in your life and want to understand the purpose for the pain?

I am available to stand in agreement with you through prayer.

There is power in agreement. To leave a prayer request, visit:

heatherbarfieldministries.com/prayer-requests

I will be praying for you.

www.ingramcontent.com/pod-product-compliance
Lightning Source LLC
Chambersburg PA
CBHW050737030426
42336CB00012B/1612